THE ART
OF AUDUBON

THE ART OF AUDUBON

The Complete Birds and Mammals

JOHN JAMES AUDUBON

With an Introduction by Roger Tory Peterson

Times
BOOKS

Published by TIMES BOOKS, a division
of Quadrangle/The New York Times Book Co., Inc.
Three Park Avenue, New York, N.Y. 10016

Published simultaneously in Canada by
Fitzhenry & Whiteside, Ltd., Toronto.

Copyright © 1979 by Volaire Ltd.

Library of Congress Cataloging in Publication Data

Audubon, John James, 1785–1851.
  The art of Audubon.

  Includes index.
    1. Birds—North America—Pictorial works.
  2. Mammals—North America—Pictorial works.
  I. Title.
  QL681.A96 1979   599'.09'70222   79-51434
  ISBN 0-8129-0841-4

Manufactured in the United States of America.

Contents

BIRDS BY FAMILY

MAMMALS BY GENUS

Introduction

Although John James Audubon was an emigre from France when he came to the United States at the age of eighteen, he was actually born in the West Indies in the year 1785. His mother was a genteel French-Creole lady and his father a prosperous French sea-captain, who after reverses in Les Cayes in Santo Domingo, now Haiti, where he owned an estate, returned to France. There the youthful Jean Jacques Fougere Audubon received a young gentleman's tutoring and even studied drawing under the guidance of the master, Jacques Louis David.

Audubon's odyssey in North America has been recounted many times; how his father sent him to his farm at Mill Grove near Philadelphia, and later set him up in business in Kentucky where he met with successive business failures as he moved westward to the Mississippi and then down to New Orleans. There his devoted wife, Lucy, supported herself and their two sons while her wandering husband was away many months at a time exploring the wilderness, painting, and prodigiously pursuing his dream of producing the epic work on the birds of North America.

Elemental forces were at work within Audubon—the stuff of which artists, poets and prophets are made. Birds were the hub around which his world revolved; their furious pace of living, their beauty, their mystery, reflected the subtle forces that guided his own life.

He was unworldly, yet closely attuned to the natural world. His simplicity, tremendous vitality, enthusiasm for life in all its variety, and his drive for creative excellence made him one of the most enduring personalities in American history.

Audubon's portraits of birds, the product of more than thirty years of field work and labor at the drawing board, were engraved by Robert Havell, Jr. of London who undertook the herculean eleven-year task of reproduction and even introduced minor changes of his own into some of the compositions and backgrounds. They were published as "The Birds of America" in four huge volumes (the largest weighing 56 pounds) between the years of 1827 and 1838. In his 435 color plates, Audubon depicted the birds exactly the size of life. Even the oversize format, known as "double elephant folio," the largest ever attempted in the history of book publishing, was insufficient to accommodate the large birds comfortably, with the result that tall birds such as the flamingo and the great blue heron are shown with their long necks drooped toward their feet. On the other hand, tiny birds like kinglets and hummingbirds are all but lost on the page.

Although Audubon's immortality rests largely on his work as an artist, he was no less of an ornithologist. The extraordinary amount of observation detailed in his five-volume, three thousand-page *Ornithological Biography,* edited and rewritten in part by William Mac-Gillivray and published almost concurrently with his *Birds of America* between the years of 1831 and 1839 as a supplemental descriptive text relating to the plates, remains as the baseline for comparing the status of birds then and now. No less important as an historical record are the comments they contain on places, people and customs.

Later, Audubon prepared a seven-volume octavo edition of his *Birds of America,* adding 65 more color plates and incorporating the text from his *Ornithological Biography.* This first octavo edition was published in New York and Philadelphia between the years of 1840 and 1844.

In reviewing Audubon's massive tour-de-force, his paintings seem to fall into at least three categories. We usually think of Audubon's style as patternistic or decorative on an open white background. Actually, the leaves, flowers and other accessories were often painted in by apprentice artists, notably Joseph Mason and George Lehman. At a later period he produced many bird portraits with solid environmental backgrounds, usually southern scenes, which were executed largely by Lehman. Among the last few plates and the 65 additional ones included in the later octavo edition are birds from the western part of the country. These are perhaps his least successful efforts. He may have grown tired of his seemingly endless projects, but a fairer judgment is that he had seen few of these birds in life. They are drawn from specimens sent to him by Nuttall, Swainson, Townsend, and Gould.

It was inevitable that after he had painted and described all the birds then known from North America, Audubon would apply his brush and pen to the mammals with which he also had a lifelong intimacy.

In the Harvard University Library there is a crayon sketch of a marmot dashed off by Audubon when he revisited France at the age of twenty. It is believed to be his earliest drawing of a mammal. Even when he was deeply involved with his bird portraiture he occasionally found time to draw mammals. A recurrent theme was an otter in a trap, which he painted again and again both in watercolor and in oils, particularly when he was in need of funds. A particularly skilled version was hung in an exhibition at the Scottish Academy.

Actually, Audubon conceived the idea of a comparable mammal publication several years earlier during conversations with the Reverend John Bachman of South Carolina, himself a naturalist of considerable scholarship, who warned Audubon of the technical problems they faced. He emphasized that mammals, because of their more secretive habits, would be more difficult to paint and to write about than birds. It was agreed that Bachman would act as co-author and editor of the three biographical volumes which were to accompany the three-volume folio of mammal portraits. The whole enterprise was impressively titled *The Viviparous Quadrupeds of North America.*

Audubon's two grown sons, John and Victor, had become full-fledged assistants in the production of his *Birds of America* by 1836. Both were learning to paint creditably, and John Woodhouse Audubon in particular gave promise of a talent that could equal his father's. The two boys married the two elder daughters of the Reverend Bachman, a family merger that was to end tragically when John's wife Maria, then 23, died of tuberculosis, leaving two small children. She was followed in death less than a year later by Victor's wife, Mary Eliza, plunging Audubon into the greatest grief he had known since the death of his own two infant daughters.

Bachman felt it was very important that Audubon, then in his late fifties, should go west to investigate some of the mammals of the frontier. His trip in 1843 to the headwaters of the Missouri and the mouth of the Yellowstone was his last great field expedition. After risking death at the hands of Sioux and Assiniboines and other adventures, he returned to his New York City estate, Minniesland, where he devoted his waning energies to the ·*Quadrupeds* which were to be published by J. T. Bowen of Philadelphia. His eyes and his mind were no longer equal to the strain, so in 1846 he began to rely more on his two talented sons. He had already painted more than 100 of the 150 colorplates. His son John painted the rest under close supervision while Victor skillfully put in the backgrounds. The remainder of the biographies were entirely the work of Reverend Bachman.

Audubon did not live to see the *Quadrupeds* completed. He died in 1851 at the age of 66.

Audubon might rightly have been called the "Father of American Ornithology" had not the Scot, Alexander Wilson, preceded him by about twenty years in the publication of his own *American Ornithology.* Although Wilson was able to find a publisher in the United States, Audubon had to go to England to find backers and printers for his larger, more ambitious folio of paintings. A total of about 190 sets were eventually bound and distributed. Less than half exist today; the others were acquired by dealers who broke them up and sold the prints individually.

Twelve years after Audubon's death, his widow sold his original paintings to the New York Historical Society where they can be seen to this day, forever safeguarded.

Audubon was the epitome of the hunter-naturalist. Modern critics sometimes point out that as a young man he found too much delight in shooting birds; he was "in blood up to his elbows." This is abundantly borne out by his *Ornithological Biography* in which he details the number of specimens he took, often far more than he needed for his portraits or his anatomical studies.

It would therefore seem inappropriate that the foremost conservation organization in the United States should adopt his name, but not so. Actually, Audubon was ahead of his time. Like so many thoughtful sportsmen since, he eventually developed a conservation conscience. In an era when there were no game laws, no national parks or refuges, when vulnerable nature gave way to human pressures and often sheer stupidity, when there was no environmental ethic, he was a witness who sounded the alarm. He became more and more concerned during his later travels when, with the perspective of his years, he could see the trend. He wrote vividly and passionately about what he saw and some of the passages in his writings were very prophetic.

Today Audubon, who wished to be known primarily as an artist, is considered the patron saint of American wildlife conservation. His name, long synonymous with birds, has become a symbol of our need to understand the environment and to live in harmony with all that is natural.

And as long as our civilization lasts, America will be in debt to this genius.

Roger Tory Peterson

PUBLISHER'S NOTE

One of the last major publishing projects on which John James Audubon embarked was the complete Octavo edition of his paintings. Containing 500 engravings of birds, partially revised from the original "double elephant folio" edition, the Octavo edition was finally published in seven volumes in the 1840s. Until now, the Octavo edition of Audubon's birds together with his 150 engravings of *Quadrupeds* have never been assembled and published in a single volume.

The bird and mammal sections have been separately arranged in a logical pattern to provide clear comparison within each individual species. Following a scientific order originally devised by Audubon, the publisher has divided the bird engravings by family and sub-divided them by genus. With each individual genus, the birds have been alphabetically positioned according to the first name on the engraving. The mammals have been grouped by Latin genus name, and the genus names have subsequently been alphabetized.

Over the years many changes have been made in Audubon's scientific names. For example, *Bison Americanus* is now *Bison Bison;* *Ursa Ferox* is now *Ursa Horribilis.* Also, Audubon divided the cats into two classifications *(Felis* and *Lynx),* a distinction that is no longer in use. There are undoubtedly many other changes which have come about in scientific nomenclature since the 1840s, but this new edition is as close to Audubon's original designations as is possible.

At the end of the volume, two indices have been provided, separately listing the birds and mammals within an English-Latin and Latin-English context.

BOOK OF BIRDS

Pl. 3

Drawn from Nature by J.J. Audubon F.R.S.F.L.S.

Black Vulture or Carrion Crow.

Lith. printed & Col.d by J.T. Bowen, Philad.a

Californian Turkey Vulture

Drawn from Nature by J. J. Audubon, F.R.S.F.L.S.   Lith.ᵈ printed & Col.ᵈ by J. T. Bowen, Phil.ᵃ

Red.-headed   Turkey   Vulture.

Drawn from Nature by J.J.Audubon, F.R.S.F.L.S.   Lith. printed & Cold by J.T.Bowen, Phila.

Caracara Eagle

Drawn from Nature by J. J. Audubon, F.R.S.F.L.S.   Lith.d printed & Col.d by J. T. Bowen, Phil.a

Broad-winged Buzzard.

Drawn from Nature by J.J.Audubon.F.R.S.F.L.. Lithᵈ Printed & Colᵈ by J.T.Bowen.Philadᵃ

Common Buzzard.

COMMON BUZZARD.

Drawn from Nature by J.J.Audubon. F.R.S.F.L.S.

Harlan's Buzzard.

Drawn from Nature by J.J.Audubon, F.R.S.F.L.S.   Lithd Printed & Cold by J. T. Bowen, Philad.ª

Harris's   Buzzard

Drawn from Nature By J.J.Audubon, F.R.S.F.L.S.   Lith.ᵈ painted & Col.ᵈ by J.T Bowen, Phil.ᵃ

Red-shouldered Buzzard

Drawn from Nature by J.J.Audubon,FRSFLS.   Lithª Printed & Colᵈby J. T. Bowen, Philadª

Red-tailed Buzzard.

Drawn from Nature by J.J.Audubon, F.R.S.F.L.S.   Lith⁴ Printed & Col⁴ by J. T. Bowen, Philad⁴

Pl. II.

R.F.
Rough-legged Buzzard.

Drawn from nature by J.J.Audubon F.R.S.F.L.S.

Lithd Printed & Cold by J.T. Bowen, Philada

Golden Eagle.

Drawn from Nature by J.J.Audubon.F.R.S.F.L.S. Lith.ª Printed & Col.ᵈby J T Bowen,Philad.ª

Pl. 10.

Washington Sea Eagle.

Drawn from Nature by J.J.Audubon F.R.S. F.L.S

Lith⁴ Printed & Col⁴ by J.T. Bowen Philad⁴

Pl. 14.

N° 3.

White-headed Sea Eagle, or Bald Eagle.

Drawn from Nature by J.J.Audubon. F.R.S.F.L.S.

Lith.d Printed & Col.d by J.T. Bowen, Philad.a

16

Common Osprey. Fish Hawk!

Drawn from Nature by J.J.Audubon.F.R.S.F.L.S.   Lith.d Printed & Col.d by J.T.Bowen.Philad.a

Black-shouldered Elanus.

Drawn from Nature by J.J.Audubon.F.R.S.F.L.S.   Lith⁴ Printed & Col⁴ by J.T.Bowen.Philad⁴

Mississipi Kite.

Drawn from Nature by J.J.Audubon. F.R.S.F.L.S.   Lithd Printed & Cold by J.T. Bowen. Philada

N° 4

Pl. 18

Swallow-tailed Hawk.

Lith.d Printed & Col.d by J.T. Bowen, Philad.a

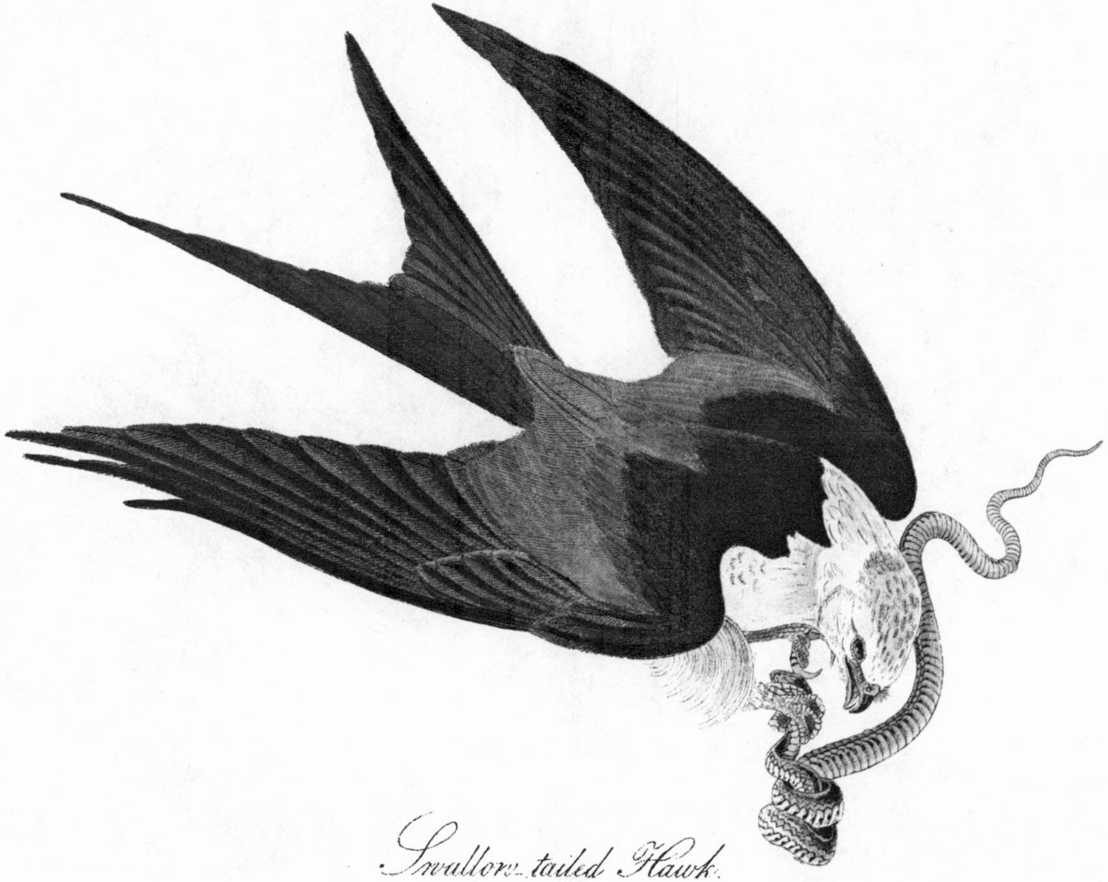

Iceland or Gyr Falcon.

Drawn from nature by J.J.Audubon, F.R.S.F.L.S.   Lith.ª Printed & Col.ª by J.T.Bowen, Philad.ª

Pl. 20

Peregrine Falcon.

Drawn from Nature by J.J.Audubon. F.R.S.FL.S.

Lith. Printed & col.d by J.T. Bowen, Philad.a

Pigeon Falcon!

Drawn from Nature by J.J.Audubon F.R.S.F.L.S   Lith.ᵈ Printed & Col.ᵈ by J.T.Bowen Phila.ᵈ

Sparrow Falcon.

Drawn from Nature by J.J.Audubon, F.R.S.F.L.S.   Lith⁴ Printed & Col⁴ by J.T.Bowen,Philad⁴

Goshawk.

Drawn from Nature by J.J.Audubon, F.R.S.F.L.S.   Lith.d Printed & Col.d by J.T. Bowen Philad.a

Cooper's Hawk.

Drawn from Nature by J.J. Audubon, F.R.S. F.L.S.   Lith.ᵈ Printed & Col.ᵈ by J.T. Bowen, Philad.ᵃ

Sharp-shinned Hawk.

Drawn from Nature by J.J.Audubon.F.R.S.F.L.S.

Lith.ᵈ Printed & Col.ᵈ by J.T.Bowen,Philad.ᵃ

Common Harrier.

Drawn from Nature by J.J.Audubon, F.R.S.F.L.S.   Lithd. Printed & Cold. by J. T. Bowen, Philad.

Burrowing Day-Owl.

Drawn from Nature by J.J.Audubon,F.R.S.F.L.S   Lith.ᵈ Printed & Col.ᵈ by J.T.Bowen.Philad.ᵃ

Columbian Day-Owl.

Drawn from Nature by J.J.Audubon.F.R.S.F.L.S   Lithd Printed & Cold by J.T.Bowen Philad.

Hawk Owl.

Drawn from Nature by J.J.Audubon, F.R.S.F.L.S.

Lith.d Printed & Col.d by J.T.Bowen, Philad.a

Passerine Day-Owl.

Drawn from Nature by J.J.Audubon.F.R.S.F.L.S.   Lithᵈ Printed & Colᵈ by J.T.Bowen.Philadᵃ

Snowy Owl.

Drawn from Nature by J.J.Audubon, F.R.S.F.L.S.   Lithd Printed & Cold by J.T.Bowen.Philadª

Little or Acadian Owl

Common Mouse

Drawn from Nature by J.J.Audubon,F.R.S.F.L.S.   Lith⁴ Printed & Col⁴by J. T. Bowen, Philad⁴

Tengmalm's Night Owl.

Drawn from Nature by J.J.Audubon. F.R.S.F.L.S.   Lith.ᵈ Printed & Col.ᵈ by J.T.Bowen, Philad.ᵃ

Barn Owl.

Drawn from Nature by J.J.Audubon,F.R.S.F.L.S.   Lithᵈ Printed & Colᵈ by J. T. Bowen, Philadᵃ

Barred Owl.

Drawn from Nature by J.J.Audubon, F.R.S.F.L.S.   Lith.ᵈ Printed & Col.ᵈ by J. T. Bowen, Philad.ᵃ

Great Cinereous Owl.

Drawn from Nature by J.J.Audubon,F.R.S.F.L.S.   Lith.ᵈ Printed & Col.ᵈ by J. T. Bowen, Philad.ᵃ

Long-eared Owl.

Drawn from Nature by J.J.Audubon, F.R.S.F.L.S.   Lith.d Printed & Col.d by J.T.Bowen, Philad.a

Short-eared Owl.

Drawn from Nature by J.J.Audubon.F.R.S.F.L.S.   Lithᵈ Printed & Colᵈ by J.T.Bowen.Philadᵃ

R.T.

Little Screech Owl.
Jersey Pine. Pinus inops

Drawn from Nature by J.J Audubon F.R.S F.L.S

Lith.d Printed & Col.d by J.T Bowen, Philad.a

Great Horned-Owl.

Drawn from Nature by J.J.Audubon,F.R.S.F.L.S.   Lith.ª Printed & Col.ª by J.T.Bowen, Philad.ª

Chuck-will's Widow,
(Harlequin Snake)

Drawn from Nature by J.J.Audubon, F.R.S.F.L.S.

Lithd Printed & Cold by J.T.Bowen, Philada

Pl.495.

Drawn from Nature by J.J.Audubon F.R.S.F.L.S

Nuttall's Whip-poor-will
Male

Lith. Printed & Col.d by J.T.Bowen, Philad.a

44

Whip-poor-will

Black Oak or Quercitron. Quercus tinctoria.

Drawn from Nature by J.J.Audubon,F.R.S.F.L.S.   Lith.ª Printed & Col.ª by J. T. Bowen, Philad.ª

Night Hawk.
White Oak. Quercus Alba.

Drawn from Nature by J.J.Audubon.F.R.S.F.L.S.   Lith.ᵈ Printed & Col.ᵈ by J.T.Bowen.Philad.ᵃ

American Swift.
(Nests.)

Drawn from Nature by J.J.Audubon.F.R.S.F.L.S.   Lithᵈ Printed & Colᵈ by J.T.Bowen.Philadᵃ

Bank Swallow

Drawn from Nature by J.J.Audubon.F.R.S.F.L.S.   Lithd Printed & Cold by J.T.Bowen.Philada

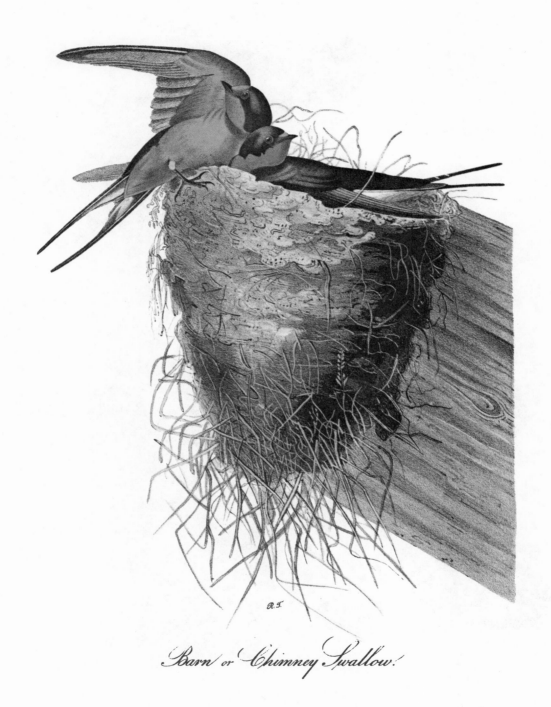

R. T.

Barn or Chimney Swallow!

Drawn from Nature by J.J.Audubon F.R.S. F.L.   Lith.d Printed & Col.d by J.T.Bowen,Philad.a

R.T.

Cliff Swallow.
(Nests.)

Drawn from Nature by J.J.Audubon. F.R.S.F.L.S.   Lithᵈ Printed & Colᵈ by J.T.Bowen, Philadᵃ

Purple Martin.
(Calabash.)

Drawn from Nature by J.J.Audubon.F.R.S.F.L.S.   Lithᵈ Printed & Colᵈ by J.T.Bowen.Philadᵃ

Rough-winged Swallow.

Drawn from Nature by J.J.Audubon.F.R.S.F.L.S.   Lith.ᵈ Printed & Col.ᵈ by J.T.Bowen,Philad.ᵃ

R. 9

Violet-Green Swallow.

Drawn from Nature by J.J.Audubon.F.R.S.F.L.   Lith.d Printed & Col.d by J.T.Bowen,Philad.a

White-bellied Swallow.

Drawn from Nature by J.J.Audubon.F.R.S.F.L.S. Lith⁴ Printed & Col⁴ by J.T.Bowen.Philad⁴

American Redstart.

Virginian Hornbeam or Iron-wood Tree.

1. Male ? Female.

Drawn from Nature by J.J.Audubon, F.R.S.F.L.S.   Lith.d Printed & Col.d by J. T. Bowen, Philad.a

Arkansaw Flycatcher.

Drawn from Nature by J.J.Audubon, F.R.S.F.L.S.   Lithᵈ Printed & Colᵈ by J.T.Bowen, Philadᵃ

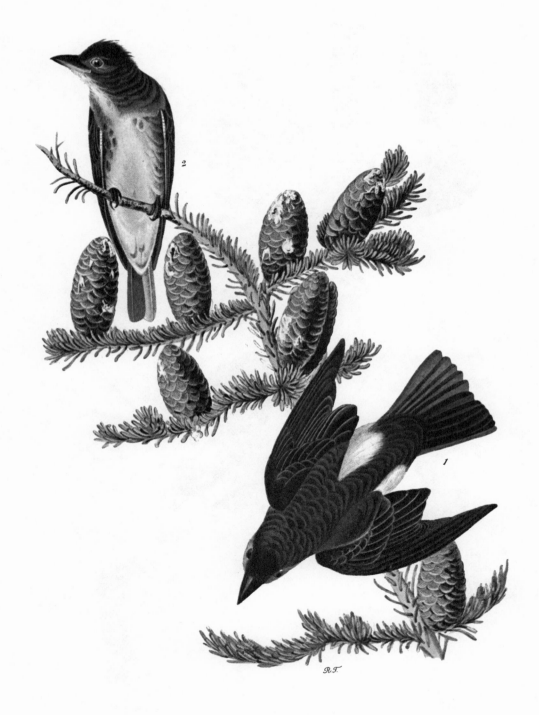

Cooper's Flycatcher.
(Balsam or Silver Fir. Pinus Balsamea.)

1 Male. 2 Female.

Drawn from Nature by J.J.Audubon, F.R.S.F.L.S.   Lithd Printed & Cold by J.T.Bowen, Philadª

Great Crested Flycatcher.

Drawn from Nature by J.J. Audubon, F.R.S. F.L.S.   Lith.ᵈ Printed & Col.ᵈ by J.T. Bowen, Philadᵃ

R.T.

Least Flycatcher
Male.

Drawn from Nature by J.J.Audubon,F.R.S.F.L.S.   Lith. Printed & Col.d by J.T. Bowen, Philad.a

Least Pewee Flycatcher.
White Oak. Quercus Prinus.
Male.

Drawn from Nature by J.J.Audubon.F.R.S.F.L.S   Lith⁴ Printed & Col⁴ by J.T.Bowen Phila⁴

Pewee Flycatcher.
Cotton Plant. Gossypium. Herbaceum.
1 Male 2 Female

Drawn from Nature by J.J.Audubon.F.R.S.F.L.S.   Lithᵈ Printed & Colᵈ by J.T.Bowen.Philad

R. 5.

Pipiry Flycatcher.
Agati Grandiflora.

Drawn from Nature by J.J.Audubon.F.R.S.F.L.S.

Lithᵈ Printed & Colᵈ by J.T.Bowen.Philadᵃ

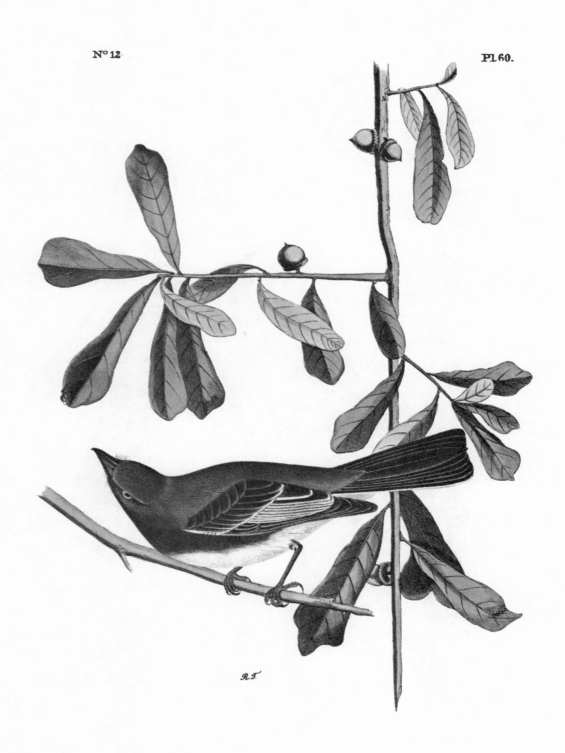

Rocky Mountain Flycatcher.
(Swamp Oak. Quercus Aquatica.)
Male

Drawn from Nature by J.J. Audubon. F.R.S. F.L.S.

Lithd Printed & Cold by J.T. Bowen. Philada

Say's Flycatcher.

1. Male. 2. Female.

Drawn from Nature by J.J.Audubon.F.R.S.F.L.S.   Lith? Printed & Col? by J.T Bowen.Phila?

Small Green-crested Flycatcher!
Sassafras. Laurus Sassafras

1 Male. 2 Female.

Drawn from Nature by J.J.Audubon.F.R.S.F.L.S.

Lith.d Printed & Col.d by J.T.Bowen.Philad.a

R.T.

Short-legged Pewit Flycatcher.
(*Hobble Bush. Viburnum Lantanoides*)
Male

Drawn from Nature by J.J.Audubon. F.R.S.F.L.S   Lithd. Printed & Cold by J.T.Bowen. Philada.

Small-headed Flycatcher
Virginian Spider-wort. Tradescantia virginica.
Male

Drawn from Nature by J.J.Audubon.F.R.S.F.L.S.   Lithᵈ Printed & Colᵈ by J.T.Bowen.Philadª

Pl.65.

Traill's Flycatcher
Sweet Gum Liquidambar Styraciflua

Male

Drawn from Nature by J. J. Audubon F.R.S.F.L.S.

Lith⁰ Printed & Col⁰ by J. T. Bowen Philad⁰

Tyrant Flycatcher or King Bird.
Cotton-wood. Populus candicans.

Drawn from Nature by J.J.Audubon.F.R.S.F.L.S.   Lith⁴ Printed & Col⁴ by J.T. Bowen Phil⁴ᵃ

Wood Pewee Flycatcher
Swamp Honeysuckle. Azalea Viscosa.

Male

Drawn from Nature by J.J.Audubon. F.R.S.F.L.S.   Lith⁴ Printed & Col⁴ by J.T. Bowen. Phila⁴

WEH.

Yellow-bellied Flycatcher.

Male

Drawn from Nature by J.J.Audubon, F.R.S.F.L.S   Lith. Printed & Col.d by J.T.Bowen, Philad.a

Fork-tailed Flycatcher.
Gordonia Lasianthus.

Drawn from Nature by J.J.Audubon.F.R.S.F.L.S.

Lith.d Printed & Col.d by J.T.Bowen.Philad.a

Swallow-tailed Flycatcher.

Drawn from Nature by J.J.Audubon,F.R.S.F.L.S.   Lith. Printed & Cold by J.T.Bowen.Philadª

Townsend's Ptilogonys.
Female.

Drawn from Nature by J.J.Audubon. F.R.S.F.L.S.

Lithᵈ Printed & Colᵈ by J.T.Bowen. Philadᵃ

Blue-grey Flycatcher.

Black Walnut. Juglans nigra.

1. Male. 2. Female.

Drawn from Nature by J.J.Audubon.F.R.S.F.L.S.   Lith⁴ Printed & Col⁴ by J.T.Bowen Philad⁴

R.T.

Bonaparte's Flycatching - Warbler?
Great Magnolia. Magnolia Grandiflora.
Male.

Drawn from Nature by J.J.Audubon, F.R.S.F.L.S.   Lith⁴ Printed & Col⁴ by J.T.Bowen, Philad⁴

Canada Flycatcher.
Great Laurel Rhododendron maximum

1. Male 2. Female.

Drawn from Nature by J.J.Audubon.F.R.S.F.L.S.   Lithᵈ Printed & Colᵈ by J.T.Bowen.Philadᵃ

Hooded Flycatching Warbler.

Erithryna herbacea.

1. Male. 2. Female.

Drawn from Nature by J.J. Audubon, P.R.S.F.L.S   Lith? Printed & Col? by J.T. Bowen, Philad?

Kentucky Flycatching-Warbler.
Magnolia auriculata

1 *Male.* 2 *Female.*

Drawn from Nature by J. J. Audubon, F.R.S.F.L.S.   Lith.d Printed & Col.d by J. T. Bowen, Philad.a

Wilson's Flycatching-Warbler.
Snakes' Head. Chelone Glabra.

1. Male. 2. Female.

Drawn from Nature by J.J.Audubon.F.R.S.F.L.S.   Lith.d Printed & Col.d by J.T.Bowen.Philad.a

Audubon's Wood-Warbler.
Strawberry Tree. Euonymus Americanus.
1. Male. 2. Female.

Drawn from Nature by J.J.Audubon.F.R.S.F.L.S.   Lithd Printed & Cold by J.T Bowen.Philad.ª

Bay-breasted Wood-Warbler
Highland Cotton-plant. Gossipium herbaceum.
1. Male 2. Female.

Drawn from Nature by J.J.Audubon, F.R.S.F.L.S.   Lithᵈ Printed & Colᵈ by J.T.Bowen. Philadᵃ

Black & yellow Wood-Warbler.
1. Male. 2. Female. 3. Young.
Flowering Raspberry. Rubus odoratus.

Drawn from Nature by J. J. Audubon, F.R.S.F.L.S.   Lith⁴ Printed & Col⁴ by J. T. Bowen, Philad⁴

Blackburnian Wood-Warbler

1. Male. 2. Female.

Phlox maculata.

Drawn from Nature by J.J.Audubon, F.R.S.F.L.S.

Lithd Printed & Cold by J.T.Bowen, Philadª

Black-poll Wood Warbler.
Black Gum Tree. Nyssa aquatica.
1. Males. 2. Female.

Drawn from Nature by J.J.Audubon.F.R.S.F.L.S.   Lith.ᵈ Printed & Col.ᵈ by J.T.Bowen.Philad.ᵃ

1.

2.

Black-throated Blue Wood-Warbler.

1. Male 2. Female.
Canadian Columbine

Drawn from Nature by J.J.Audubon, F.R.S.F.L.S.   Lithᵈ Printed & Colᵈ by J.T.Bowen, Philadᵃ.

Black-throated Green Wood Warbler.
Caprifolium Sempervirens
1 Male 2 Female.

Drawn from Nature by J.J.Audubon, F.R.S.F.L.S   Lith? Printed & Col? by J.T. Bowen. Philad?

Black-throated Grey Wood-Warbler.
Males.

Drawn from Nature by J.J.Audubon. F.R.S.F.L.S.   Lithd. Printed & Cold. by J.T.Bowen. Philada.

Blue Mountain Warbler.

Male

Drawn from Nature by J.J.Audubon.F.R.S.F.L.S.   Lithd Printed & Cold by J.T.Bowen.Philada

Blue yellow-backed Wood-Warbler.

1. Male. 2. Female.
Louisiana Flag.

Drawn from Nature by J.J.Audubon, F.R.S.F.L.S.   Lith⁴ Printed & Col⁴ by J.T.Bowen, Philad⁴

Cape May Wood Warbler.
1. Male 2. Female.

Drawn from Nature by J.J.Audubon.F.R.S.F.L.S.   Lith_d Printed & Col_d by J.T.Bowen,Philad_a

Chesnut-sided Wood Warbler.
Moth Mullein. Verbascum Blattaria.

1. Male. 2. Female.

Drawn from Nature by J. J. Audubon, F.R.S.F.L.S.

Lithᵈ Printᵈ & Colᵈ by J. T. Bowen Philadᵃ

Cærulean Wood-Warbler.

1. Old Male. 2. Young Male.
Bear-berry and Spanish Mulberry.

Drawn from Nature by J.J.Audubon. F.R.S. F.L.S.

Lith.d Printed & Col.d by J.T.Bowen Philad.a

Connecticut Warbler.

1. Male: 2. Female.
Gentiana Saponaria.

Drawn from Nature by J.J.Audubon, F.R.S.F.L.S   Lith⁴ Printed & Col⁴ by J.T. Bowen, Phila⁴⁵

R. T.

Hemlock Warbler
Dwarf Maple. Acer Spicatum
1. Male 2. Female.

Drawn from Nature by J.J.Audubon. F.R.S.F.L.S.   Lithd. Printed & Cold by J.T. Bowen. Philadª

R.T.

Hermit Wood-Warbler.

1. Male. 2. Female.
Strawberry Tree.

Drawn from Nature by J.J.Audubon F.R.S.F.L.S.   Lith.ᵈ Printed & Col.ᵈ by J.T.Bowen Philaᵈ.ᵃ

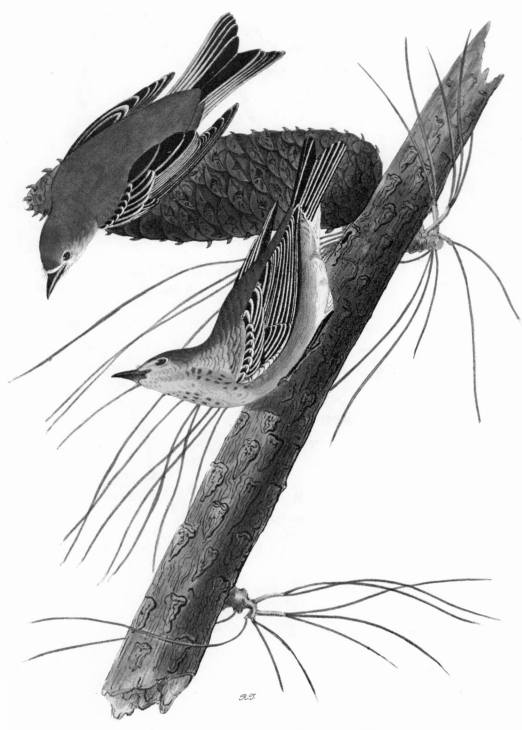

Pine-creeping Wood-Warbler
Yellow Pine. Pinus variabilis.

1. Male 2. Female.

Drawn from Nature by J.J. Audubon, F.R.S.F.L.S.   Lith⁴ Printed & Col⁴ by J.T. Bowen, Philad⁴

R.T.

Prairie Wood-Warbler.

1. Male. 2. Female.
Buffalo Grass

Drawn from Nature by J.J.Audubon.F.R.S.F.L.S.   Lithd Printed & Cold by J.T.Bowen.Philadª

Rathbone's Wood-Warbler.

1 Male. 2 Female.

Ramping Trumpet-flower?

Drawn from Nature by J.J.Audubon, F.R.S.F.L.S.   Lithd Printed & Cold by J.T.Bowen, Philada

R.T.

Townsend's Wood-Warbler.

Male.

Carolina Allspice.

Drawn from Nature by J.J.Audubon, F.R.S.F.L.S.

Lith⁴ Printed & Col⁴ by J.T Bowen Philad⁴

Yellow-crowned Wood-Warbler!

Iris versicolor.

1. Male. 2. Young.

Drawn from Nature by J.J.Audubon.F.R.S.F.L.S.   Lithd Printed & Cold by J.T.Bowen.Philada

Yellow-poll Wood-Warbler.

Males.

Drawn from Nature by J. J. Audubon, F.R.S. F.L.S.   Lithd Printed & Cold by J.T. Bowen, Philada

Yellow Red-poll Wood-Warbler.
1. *Males.* 2. *Young.*
Wild Orange Tree.

Drawn from Nature by J.J.Audubon, F.R.S.F.L.S.   Lith.d Printed & Col.d by J.T.Bowen, Philad.a

Yellow-throated Wood-Warbler.
Chinquapin. Castanea pumila.
Male.

Drawn from Nature by J. J. Audubon. F.R.S.F.L.S.   Lithd Printed & Cold by J.T.Bowen.Philada

Pl. 103.

N° 21.

R.T.

Delafield's Ground Warbler.
Male.

Drawn from Nature by J.J.Audubon. F.R.S.F.L.S.

Lith⁴ Printed & Col⁴ by J.T. Bowen, Phila⁴⁺

Macgillivray's Ground-Warbler

1. Male. 2. Female

Drawn from Nature by J.J.Audubon, F.R.S.F.L.S.   Lith.ª Printed & Col.ª by J.T.Bowen, Philad.ª

Maryland Ground-Warbler.

1 Adult Male. 2 Young Male. 3 Female

Bitter-wood Tree Viburnum prunifolium.

Drawn from Nature by J.J.Audubon, F.R.S.F.L.S   Lith.d Printed & Col.d by J.T. Bowen, Philad.a

Mourning Ground-Warbler.

Male.

Pheasant's-eye Flos Adonis.

Drawn from Nature by J.J Audubon, F.R.S.F.L.S.   Lith.ᵈ Printed & Col.ᵈ by J.T. Bowen, Philad.ᵃ

Bachman's Swamp-Warbler.
1. Male. 2 Female
Gordonia pubescens.

Drawn from Nature by J.J.Audubon.F.R.S.F.L.S.

Lithd Printed & Cold by J.T.Bowen.Philadª

1.

2.

Blue-winged Yellow Swamp-Warbler.
1. Male 2. Female
Cotton Rose. Hibiscus grandiflorus.

Drawn from Nature by J.J.Audubon.F.R.S.F.L.S.   Lithd. Printed & Cold. by J.T.Bowen. Philad.

R.T.

Carbonated Swamp-Warbler

Males

May-bush or Service. Pyrus Botryapium.

Drawn from Nature by J.J. Audubon, F.R.S. F.L.S.   Lithd Printed & Cold by J.T. Bowen Philadª

Golden-winged Swamp-Warbler.

1 Male. 2 Female.

Drawn from Nature by J. J. Audubon, F.R.S.F.L.S.   Lithd Printed & Cold by J. T. Bowen, Philada

R.T.

Nashville Swamp-Warbler
1. Male. 2. Female
Swamp Spice Ilex prinoides

Drawn from Nature by J.J.Audubon. F.R.S.F.L.S.   Lith.ᵈ Printed & Col.ᵈ by J.T. Bowen, Philadª

Orange-crowned Swamp Warbler.

1. Male. 2. Female.
Huckleberry. Vaccinium frondosum.

Drawn from Nature by J. J. Audubon, F. R. S. F. L. S.   Lith.ᵈ Printed & Col.ᵈ by J. T. Bowen, Philad.ª

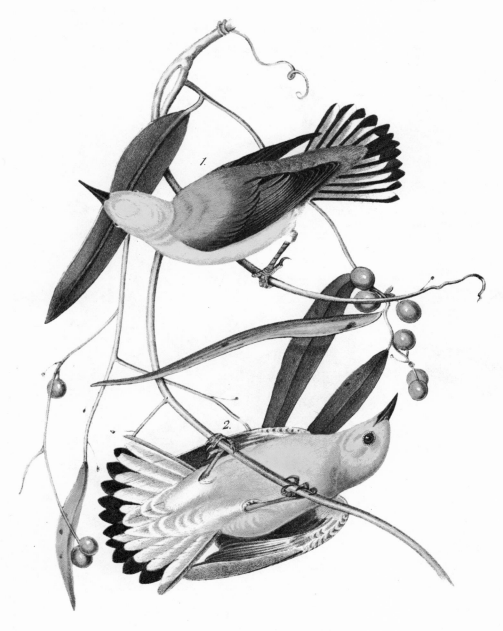

R.T.

Prothonotary Swamp-Warbler.

1. Male. 2. Female.

Cane Vine

Drawn from Nature by J.J.Audubon, F.R.S.F.L.S.   Lith⁴ Printed & Col⁴ by J.T.Bowen, Philad⁴

2.5.

Swainson's Swamp Warbler.
Male.
Orange-coloured Azalea. Azalea calendulacea

Drawn from Nature by J.J. Audubon. F.R.S.F.L.S.   Lithᵈ Printed & Colᵈ by J.T. Bowen. Philadᵃ

R.T.

Tennessee Swamp Warbler.

Male

Ilex laxiflora

Drawn from Nature by J.J.Audubon, F.R.S.F.L.S.   Lith.ᵈ Printed & Col.ᵈ by J.T.Bowen, Philad.ᵃ

Worm-eating Swamp Warbler.
1. Male. 2. Female.
American Poke-weed. Phytolacca decandra.

Drawn from Nature by J.J.Audubon, F.R.S.F.L.S.   Lithd Printed & Cold by J.T.Bowen, Philadª

R.T.

Black-and-white Creeping Warbler

Male.

Black Larch. Pinus pendula.

Drawn from Nature by J.J.Audubon, F.R.S.F.L.S.   Lith.ᵈ Printed & Col.ᵈ by J.T.Bowen, Philadᵃ

Brown Tree-creeper

1 Male 2.Female

Drawn from Nature by J.J.Audubon.F.R.S.F.L.S.   Lith⁴ Printed & Col⁴ by J.T.Bowen.Philad⁴

Bewicks Wren

Male.

Iron-wood Tree

Drawn from Nature by J.J.Audubon.F.R.S.F.L.S.   Lithᵈ Printed & Colᵈ by J.T.Bowen.Philadᵃ

Great Carolina Wren?

1. Male. 2. Female.

Dwarf Buck-eye. Æsculus. Pavia?

Drawn from Nature by J.J.Audubon, F.R.S.F.L.S.   Lith.ᵈ Printed & Col.ᵈ by J. T. Bowen, Philad.ᵗ

Marsh Wren

1. Males 2 Female and Nest

Drawn from Nature by J. J. Audubon. F.R.S. F.L.S.   Lith. Printed & Col.ᵈ by J. T. Bowen, Philad.ᵃ

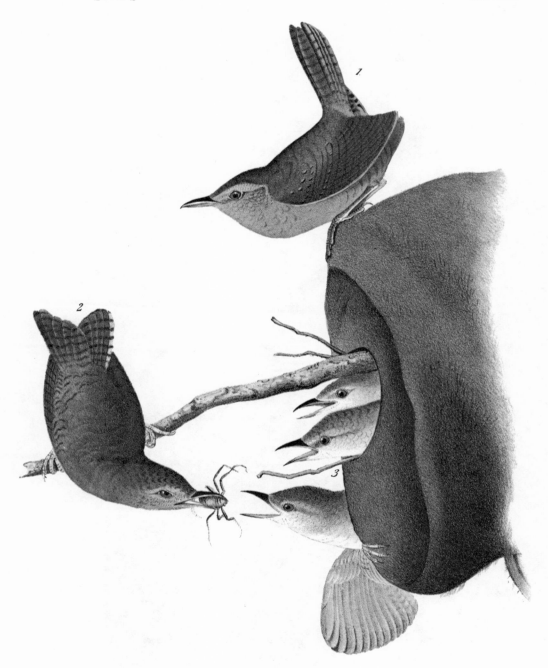

R.T.

House Wren

1. Male.   2. Female. 3. Young.
In an old Hat.

Drawn from Nature by J.J.Audubon. F.R.S.F.L.S.   Lith.ᵈ Printed & Col.ᵈ by J.T. Bowen, Philad.ᵃ

Parkman's Wren.

Male.
Pogonia divaricata

Drawn from Nature by J. J. Audubon F.R.S F.L.S.   Lithd Printed & Cold by J. T. Bowen, Philada

Rock - Wren
Adult Female
Smilacina borealis

Drawn from Nature by J.J.Audubon.F.R.S.F.L.S.   Lith.ᵈ Printed & Col.ᵈ by J.T.Bowen.Philad.ᵃ

Short-billed Marsh Wren.

1. Male. 2. Female and Nest.

Drawn from Nature by J.J. Audubon F.R.S. F.L.S   Lith.ᵈ Printed&Col.ᵈ by J.T. Bowen Philad.ᵃ

Winter Wren.

1. Male. 2. Female. 3. Young.

Drawn from Nature by J.J. Audubon, F.R.S.F.L.S.

Lithd. Printed & Cold by J.T. Bowen, Philadª.

Wood Wren

Male.

Arbutus. Uva-ursi.

Drawn from Nature by J.J.Audubon, F.R.S.F.L.S.   Lith.d Printed & Col.d by J.T.Bowen,Philad.a

Black cap Titmouse
1. Male 2 Female
Sweet Brian.

Drawn from Nature by J.J.Audubon F.R.S.F.L.S.

Lith. Printed & Col. by J.T.Bowen Philad.

Pl 127.

1

2

Carolina Titmouse.

1. Male. 2. Female.

Plant. Supple Jack.

Drawn from Nature by J. J. Audubon F.R.S.E.L.S.

Lith⁴ Printed & Col⁴ by J. T. Bowen. Philad⁴

Chesnut-backed Titmouse.

1. Male. 2. Female.

Chesnut-crowned Titmouse

1. Male. 2. Female and Nest.

Drawn from Nature by J.J.Audubon, F.R.S.F.L.S.   Lith.ᵈ Printed & Col.ᵈ by J.T.Bowen, Philad.ᵃ

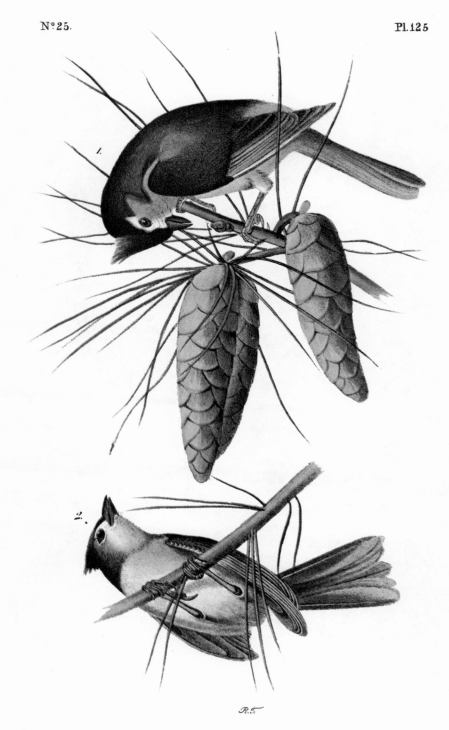

R.T.

Crested Titmouse

1. Male 2.Female.
White Pine. Pinus Strobus

Drawn from Nature by J.J Audubon.F.R.S.F.L.S.   Lithd Printed&Cold by J.T.Bowen. Philadª

Hudson's Bay Titmouse.

1. Male. 2. Female. 3. Young.

Drawn from Nature by J.J. Audubon F.R.S.F.L.S

Lith⁴ Printed & Col⁵ by J.T. Bowen Philad⁵

R.T.

American Golden-crested Kinglet.

1. Male 2. Female.

Thalia dealbata.

Drawn from Nature by J.J.Audubon.F.R.S.F.L.S.   Lithᵈ Printed & Colᵈ by J.T.Bowen.Philadᵃ

R.F.

Cuvier's Kinglet

Male.

Broad-leaved laurel. Kalmia latifolia.

Drawn from Nature by J.J.Audubon, F.R.S.F.L.S.   Lith⁴ Printed & Col⁴ by J.T.Bowen, Philad⁴

Ruby-crowned Kinglet
1. Male. 2. Female.
Kalmia augustifolia.

Drawn from Nature by J.J.Audubon. F.R.S.F.L.S.   Lithd Printed & Cold by J.T. Bowen Philada

Arctic Blue Bird
Male 1. Female 2

Drawn from nature by J.J. Audubon F.R.S.F.L.S.   Lith & Printed by Endicott New York.

Common Blue Bird

1. Male. 2. Female. 3 Young.

Great Mullein Verbascum Thapsus.

Drawn from Nature by J.J.Audubon. F.R.S.F.L.S   Lithd Printed & Cold by J.T. Bowen, Philada

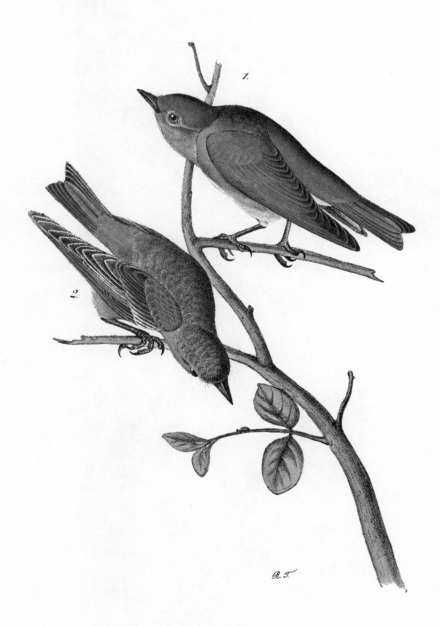

Western Blue Bird.

1. Male. 2. Female.

Drawn from Nature by J.J.Audubon.F.R.S.F.L.S.   Lithᵈ Printed & Colᵈ by J.T.Bowen.Philadᵃ

Pl. 137.

N°.28.

American Dipper
Male & Female 2.

Drawn from nature by J.J. Audubon F.R.S. FL.S.

Lith & Printed by Endicott New York

Cat Bird
Male 1 Female 2.
Plant Black-berry , Rubus villosus .

Drawn from nature by J.J. Audubon F.R.S.F.L.S.

Lith. & Printed by Endicott New York.

Common Mocking Bird
Males 1 & 2, Female 3,
Florida Jessamine, Gelseminum nitidum
Rattlesnake

Drawn from nature by J.J. Audubon F.R.S.F.L.S.

Lith. & Printed by Endicott New York.

Ferruginous Mocking Bird
Males 1,2,3, Female 4.

Drawn from nature by J.J. Audubon F.R.S.F.L.S.   Lith & Printed by Endicott New York

Mountain Mocking Bird.
Male.

Drawn from nature by J.J. Audubon F.R.S.FL.S.   Lith. & Printed by Endicott New York.

American Robin, or Migratory Thrush.
Male 1. Female 2 and young.
Chesnut Oak Quercus prinus.

Drawn from nature by J.J. Audubon F.R.S.F.L.S.   Lith. & Printed by Endicott New York.

Dwarf Thrush
Male
Plant Porcelia Triloba.

Drawn from nature by J.J. Audubon F.R.S.F.L.S.   Lith. & Printed by Endicott New York

Hermit Thrush
Male 1. Female 2.
Plant Robin Wood.

Drawn from nature by J.J. Audubon F.R.S.F.L.S.   Lith. & Printed by Endicott New York.

Tawny Thrush.
Male,

Habenaria Lacera — Cornus Canadensis

Drawn from nature by J.J. Audubon F.R.S.F.L.S.   Lith. & Printed by Endicott New York

Varied Thrush.
Male 1, Female 2.
American Mistletoe, Viscum verticillatum.

Drawn from nature by J.J Audubon F.R.S.F.L.S.   Lith. & Printed by Endicott New York.

Wood Thrush
Male 1. Female 2.
Common Dogwood.

Drawn from nature by J.J Audubon F.R.S.F.L.S   Lith. & Printed by Endicott New York

Aquatic Wood - Wagtail
Male 1 Female 2.
Plant. Indian Turnip.

Drawn from nature by J.J. Audubon F.R.S.F.L.S.   Lith & Printed by Endicott New York.

Golden Crowned Wagtail (Thrush.)
Male 1. Female 2.
Plant Woody Nightshade.

Drawn from nature by J.J Audubon F.R.S.F.L.S.   Lith. & Printed by Endicott New York

Pl. 150.

American Pipit, or Titlark.
Male 1. Female 2.

Drawn from nature by J.J. Audubon F.R.S.F.L.S.

Lith. & Printed by Endicott New York

N°31.

Pl. 151

Shore Lark.

1. Male Summer Plumage 2. Do Winter 3 Female 4 Young & Nest.

Drawn from Nature by J.J. Audubon. F.R.S.F.L.S.

Lith⁴ Printed & Col⁴ by J.T Bowen. Philad⁴.

Pl. 486.

W.E.H.

Sprague's Missouri Lark

Male

Drawn from Nature by J. J. Audubon, F.R.S. F.L.S.

Lith. Printed & Col.d by J.T. Bowen, Phila.

N°100.

Western Shore Lark

WEH

Male

Drawn from Nature by J.J.Audubon, F.R.S. F.L.S.

Lith. Printed & Col.d by J.T.Bowen, Philad.a

R.T.

Chesnut-collared Lark-Bunting.

Male.

Drawn from Nature by J.J.Audubon.F.R.S.F.L.S.   Lith⁴ Printed & Col⁴ by J.T.Bowen.Philad⁴

Pl. 152.

Lapland Lark Bunting.

1. Male Spring Plumage 2. D⁰ Winter. 3. Female.

Drawn from Nature by J.J.Audubon.F.R.S.F.L.S.

Lith:Printed & Col.ᵈ by J.T.Bowen,Philadᵃ.

R.T.

Painted Lark-Bunting.

Male.

Drawn from Nature by J.J.Audubon.F.R.S.F.L.S.   Lith.ᵈ Printed & Col.ᵈby J.T.Bowen.Philad.ᵗ

PL.487.

Smith's Lark Bunting.

Adult Male.

Drawn from Nature by J.J. Audubon, F.R.S. F.L.S

Lith. Printed & Col.ª by J.T. Bowen, Philaª

162

Snow Lark Bunting

1. 2. Adult. 3. Young.

Drawn from Nature by J.J.Audubon.F.R.S.F.L.S.   Lithᵈ Printed & Colᵈ by J.T.Bowen Philadᵃ

Pl.500.

"Baird's Bunting.
Male

Drawn from Nature by J.J. Audubon F.R.S.F.L.S.

Lith Printed & Col.d by J.T.Bowen Philad.a

R.T

Bay - winged Bunting.

Male.

Prickly Pear Cactus Opuntia

Drawn from Nature by J. J. Audubon F.R.S.F.L.S.   Lith.ᵈ Printed & Col.ᵈ by J. T. Bowen Philad.ᵃ

R. S.

Black-throated Bunting.

1. Male. 2. Female.

Phalaris arundinacea and Antirrhinum Linaria

Drawn from Nature by J.J.Audubon,F.R.S.F.L.S.   Lithd Printed & Cold by J.T.Bowen Philadª.

R.T.

Canada Bunting (Tree Sparrow.)
1. Male. 2. Female.
Canadian Barberry.

Drawn from Nature by J.J.Audubon, F.R.S.F.L.S.

Lith.ᵈ Printed & Col.ᵈ by J.T.Bowen Philad.ᵃ

R.T.

Chipping Bunting.
Male.
Black locust or False Acacia.
Robina pseudacacia.

Drawn from Nature by J.J Audubon. F.R.S.F.L.S.   Lith⁴Printed & Col⁴by J.T.Bowen. Philad⁴.

R. T.

Clay-coloured Bunting.

Male.

Asclepias tuberosa.

Drawn from Nature by J.J Audubon FRS FLS.

Lith.d Printed & Col.d by J.T Bowen. Philad.a

Pl.164.

R.T.

Field Bunting.

Male.

Calopogon pulchellus. Brown.

Dwarf Huckle-berry. Vaccinium tenellum.

Drawn from Nature by J.J. Audubon. F.R.S.F.L.S.

Lithᵈ Printed & Colᵈ by J.T. Bowen. Philadᵃ

Pl. 163.

Shape of tail.

Henslow's Bunting.
Male.
Indian Pink-root or Worm-grass.
Spigelia Marilandica
Phlox aristata.

R. T.

Lark Bunting.

Male.

Drawn from Nature by J.J.Audubon, F.R.S.F.L.S   Lithᵈ Printed & Colᵈ by J.T.Bowen Philadᵃ

Le Conti's Sharp-tailed Bunting.
Male.

Drawn from Nature by J.J.Audubon, F.R.S.F.L.S   Lith Printed & Col.d by J.T. Bowen Philad.ª

R.T.

Savannah Bunting

1. Male. 2. Female.

Indian Pink-root. Spigelia Marilandica.

Drawn from Nature by J.J.Audubon.F.R.S.F.L.S.   Lith.ª Printed & Col.ᵈ by J.T.Bowen.Philad.ª

N.E.1.

Shattucks Bunting

Male

Drawn from Nature by J.J.Audubon, F.R.S.F.L.S   Lith.Printed & Col.d by J.T.Bowen, Philad.a

R. T.

Townsend's Bunting.

Male.

Drawn from Nature by J. J. Audubon, F.R.S. F.L.S.   Lith.ᵈ Printed & Col.ᵈ by J. T. Bowen, Philadᵃ

n. 5.

Yellow-winged Bunting.

Male.

Drawn from Nature by J.J.Audubon.F.R.S.F.L.S.   Lith⁴.Printed & Col⁴ by J. T. Bowen.Philad⁴.

Common Snow-Bird.

1. Male. 2. Female

Drawn from Nature by J. J. Audubon. F.R.S.F.L.S   Lithᵈ Printed & Colᵈ by J. T. Bowen, Philadᵃ.

Oregon Snow Bird

1. Male 2. Female.
Rosa Laevigata

Drawn from Nature by J.J. Audubon F.R.S F.L.S.   Lith.d Printed & Col.d by J. T. Bowen. Philad.a

179

Indigo Bunting.

1. 2. 3. Males in different States of Plumage. 4. Female.

Wild Sarsaparilla.

Drawn from Nature by J.J.Audubon, F.R.S.F.L.S.   Lithᵈ Printed & Colᵈ by J. T. Bowen, Philadᵃ

R. T

Lazuli Finch.

1. Male 2. Female.
♂ Wild Spanish Coffee.

Drawn from Nature by J.J. Audubon F.R.S.F.L.S.   Lithᵈ Printed & Colᵈ by J. T. Bowen. Philadᵗ.

Painted Bunting

1. 2. 3. Males in different States of Plumage. 4. Female.

Chicasaw Wild Plum.

Drawn from Nature by J. J. Audubon F.R.S.F.L.S.   Lith.ᵈ Printed & Col.ᵈ by J. T. Bowen Philadᵈ

Macgillivray's Shore-Finch.

1. Male. 2. Female.

Drawn from Nature by J. J. Audubon. F.R.S.F.L.S.   Lith⁴ Printed & Col⁴ by J. T. Bowen. Philad⁴.

Pl. 172.

Sea-side Finch

1. Male 2. Female

Carolina Rose.

Drawn from Nature by J. J. Audubon, F.R.S. F.L.S.

Lithd Printed & Cold by J. T. Bowen, Philad.

R.T.

Sharp-tailed Finch.

1. *Males.* 2. *Female & Nest.*

Drawn from Nature by J.J. Audubon, F.R.S.F.L.S.   Lith.ᵈ Printed & Col.ᵈ by J. T. Bowen. Philad.ᵃ

a. T.

Swamp Sparrow
Male.
May-apple

Drawn from Nature by Mrs Lucy Audubon.   Lithd Printed & Cold by J. T. Bowen Philada

Bachman's Pinewood Finch

Male

Pinckneya pubescens.

Drawn from Nature by J.J.Audubon.FRSFLS   Lith.ᵈ Printed & Col.ᵈ by J.T.Bowen.Philadᵃ

Lincoln's Pinewood Finch.

1 Male. 2 Female.

1. Dwarf Cornel. 2. Cloudberry 3. Glaucous Kalmia.

Drawn from Nature by J.J. Audubon F.R.S.F.L.S.   Lith.ᵈ Printed & Col.ᵈ by J.T. Bowen Philad.

Lesser Redpoll Linnet.

1. Male 2. Female.

Drawn from Nature by J.J. Audubon F.R.S.E.L.S.   Lithd. Printed & Cold. by J.T. Bowen Philad.

Mealy Redpoll Linnet.

Male.

Drawn from Nature by J.J. Audubon. F.R.S. F.L.S.   Lith.d Printed & Col.d by J.T. Bowen. Philad.a

R.T.

Pine Linnet.

1 Male.2.Female

Black Larch.

Drawn from Nature by J.J.Audubon. F.R.S.F.L.S.   Lith Printed & Cold by J.T.Bowen Philad.

American Goldfinch.
1 Male. 2. Female
Common Thistle

Drawn from Nature by J.J. Audubon F.R.S.F.L.S.   Lith.ᵈ Printed & Col.ᵈ by J.T. Bowen Philad

Arkansaw Goldfinch.

Male.

Drawn from Nature by J.J. Audubon. F.R.S.F.L.S.   Lith.ᵈ Printed & Col.ᵈ by J.T. Bowen Philad.

Black-headed Goldfinch.

Male.

Drawn from Nature by J.J.Audubon.FRSFLS

Lith.ᵈ Printed & Col.ᵈ by J.T.Bowen, Philad.

Stanley Goldfinch.

Drawn from Nature by J.J. Audubon. F.R.S.F.L.S.   Lith.ᵈ Printed & Col.ᵈ by J.T. Bowen Philad.

Yarrell's Goldfinch

1 Male. 2. Female.

Drawn from Nature by J.J.Audubon. F.R.S.F.L.S.   Lith.ᵈ Printed & Col.ᵈ by J.T. Bowen. Philad.

Black-and-yellow-crowned Finch.

Drawn from Nature by J.J.Audubon.F.R.S.F.L.S.   Lithd Printed & Cold by J. T. Bowen.Philad.

Brown Finch.

Female.

Drawn from Nature by J.J.Audubon.F.R.S.F.L.S.   Lith Printed & Cold by J.T.Bowen Philad.

Pl.186.

Fox-coloured Finch

1. *Male.* 2. *Female.*

Drawn from Nature by J.J.Audubon. F.R.S.F.L.S.

Lith.ᵈ Printed & Col.ᵈ by J.T.Bowen. Phila.ᵗ

WEH

Harris' Finch

1, Adult Male. 2, Young Female.

Drawn from Nature by J.J. Audubon, F.R.S.F.L.S.

Lith Printed & Col.ᵈ by J.T. Bowen, Phila.

Song Finch

1. Male. 2. Female.

Huckle-berry, or Blue tangled Vaccinium frondosum.

Drawn from Nature by J.J.Audubon.F.R.S.F.L.S.　　　　　　Lith.ᵈ Printed & Col.ᵈ by J.T.Bowen.Philad.ᵃ

Morton's Finch.

Male.

Drawn from Nature by J.J.Audubon.F.R.S.F.L.S.   Lith.ᵈ Printed & Col.ᵈ by J.T.Bowen.Philad.

R.T.

Townsend's Finch

.Male.

Drawn from Nature by J.J.Audubon.F.R.S.F.L.S.   Lithᵈ Printed & Colᵈ by J.T.Bowen.Philadᵃ

White-crowned Finch.

1. Male. 2. Female.
Wild Summer Grape.

Drawn from Nature by J.J.Audubon,F.R.S.F.L.S.   Lith.ᵈ Printed & Col.ᵈ by J.T.Bowen Philad.ᵃ

White-throated Finch.

1. Male. 2. Female.

Common Dogwood.

Drawn from Nature by J.J.Audubon,F.R.S.F.L.S.   Lith.d Printed & Col.d by J. T. Bowen, Philad.a

Pl. 194.

1.

2.

R.T

Arctic Ground Finch.

1. Male. 2. Female.

Drawn from Nature by J. J. Audubon. F.R.S.F.L.S

Lith.d Printed & Col.d by J. T. Bowen. Philad.

Towhe Ground Finch.

1. Male. 2. Female.
Common Blackberry.

Drawn from Nature by J.J.Audubon.F.R.S.E.LS.   Lith.ª Printed & Col.ª by J.T.Bowen Philad.

Crimson-fronted Purple Finch.

Male.

Drawn from Nature by J. J. Audubon. F.R.S.F.L.S.

Lith.ᵈ Printed & Col.ᵈ by J. T. Bowen. Philad.

Crested Purple Finch.

1. *Males.* 2. *Female*

Red Larch. Larix Americana.

Drawn from Nature by J.J.Audubon, F.R.S.F.L.S.   Lith.ᵈPrinted & Col.ᵈby J. T. Bowen, Philadᵃ

Grey-crowned Purple Finch.

Male.

Stokesia cyanea

Drawn from Nature by J.J Audubon F.R.S.F.L.S.   Lith.ᵈ Printed & Col.ᵈ by J.T Bowen Philad.

Common Pine-finch.

1.__Male. 2.__Female.

Drawn from Nature by J.J.Audubon. F.R.S.F.L.S.   Lith.ᵈ, Printed & Colᵈ by J. T. Bowen Phil.

Pl. 200.

Common Crossbill.

1. Males. 2. Females.

Drawn from Nature by J. J. Audubon, F.R.S.F.L.S.

Lith.ᵈ Printed & Col.ᵈ by J. T. Bowen, Phil.

White-winged Crossbill.

1. Males. 2. Female.

Drawn from Nature by J.J.Audubon,F.R.S.F.L.S.

Lithᵈ Printed & Colᵈ by J. T. Bowen, Philadᵈ

Prairie Lark-Finch.

1. Male. 2. Female.

Drawn from Nature by J. J. Audubon. F.R.S.F.L.S.   Lithᵈ Printed & Colᵈ by J. T. Bowen. Philad.

Common Cardinal Grosbeak.

1. Male. 2. Female.

Wild Almond. Prunus caroliniana.

Drawn from Nature by J.J.Audubon.F.R.S.F.L.S.　　　　　Lith.ᵈ,Printed & Col.ᵈ by J.T.Bowen, Phil.

Pl. 206.

Black-headed Song-Grosbeak.

1. Male. 2. Female.

Blue Song Grosbeak.

1. Male. 2. Female. 3. Young.

Drawn from Nature by J. J. Audubon F.R.S.F.L.S.   Lithd Printed & Cold by J. T. Bowen Philad

Rose-breasted Song-Grosbeak.
1. Males. 2. Female. 3. Young Male.
Ground Hemlock Taxus canadensis.

Drawn from Nature by J.J.Audubon,F.R.S.F.L.S.   Lithᵈ Printed & Colᵈ by J. T. Bowen, Philadᵃ

Evening Grosbeak.

1. Male. 2. Female. 3. Young Male.

Drawn from Nature by J. J. Audubon. F.R.S.F.L.S.   Lith.ᵈ Printed & Col.ᵈ by J. T. Bowen, Philad.

Louisiana Tanager.

1. Males. 2. Female.

Drawn from Nature by J.J.Audubon,F.R.S.F.L.S.   Lith.ᵈ Printed & Col.ᵈ by J. T. Bowen, Philad.ª

Scarlet Tanager.

1. Male. 2. Female.

Drawn from Nature by J.J.Audubon.F.R.S.F.L.S.   Lith^d Printed & Col^d by J.T.Bowen.Philad.

Pl. 208.

Summer Red-bird

1. Male. 2. Female 3. Young Male.

Wild Muscadine Vitis rotundifolia. Mich

Drawn from Nature by J.J.Audubon, F.R.S.F.L.S.

Lithᵈ Printed & Colᵈ by J. T. Bowen, Philadᵃ

Wandering Rice-bird

1. Male. 2. Female.
Red Maple. Acer Rubrum.

Drawn from Nature by J.J.Audubon. F.R.S.F.L.S.   Lith.ᵈ Printed & Col.ᵈ by J. T. Bowen Philad.

223

Pl. 212.

Drawn from Nature by J.J.Audubon.F.R.S.F.L.S.

Common Cow-Bird.
1.Male. 2.Female. 3.Young.

Lith⁴Printed & Col⁴by J.T.Bowen.Philad.

Red-and-black-shouldered Marsh-Blackbird

1. Male 2. Female.

Drawn from Nature by J.J. Audubon. F.R.S. F.L.S.   Lith.ᵈ Printed & Col.ᵈ by J.T. Bowen Philad.

Red-and-white-shouldered. Marsh-Blackbird

Male.

Drawn from Nature by J.J.Audubon, F.R.S.F.L.S.   Lithd Printed & Cold by J. T. Bowen Philad

Red-winged Starling

1. Male Adult. 2. Young Male. 3. Female.

Red Maple

Drawn from Nature by J.J. Audubon. F.R.S.F.L.S.   Lith.d Printed & Col.d by J.T.Bowen. Philad.

Pl 213.

Saffron-headed Marsh-Blackbird.

1. Male. 2. Female 3. Young Male.

Drawn from Nature by J.J.Audubon.F.R.S.F.L.S.

Lith.ᵈ Printed & Col.ᵈ by J.T.Bowen.Philad.

Baltimore Oriole, or Hang-nest

1 Male adult. 2 Young Male. 3 Female.

Tulip Tree.

Drawn from Nature by J.J. Audubon. F.R.S.F.L.S.   Lith.ᵈ Printed & Col.ᵈ by J.T. Bowen. Phil.

Bullock's Troopial

1. Male Adult. 2. Young Male 3. Female

Caprifolium flavum.

Drawn from Nature by J.J. Audubon. F.R.S.F.L.S.   Lithd Printed & Cold by J. T. Bowen. Phil.

Common Troupial.

Male.

Drawn from Nature by J.J.Audubon, F.R.S.F.L.S.   Lith.ᵈ Printed & Col.ᵈ by J. T. Bowen, Philadᵃ.

Pl. 219.

Orchard Oriole or Hang-nest.
1. Male adult. 2. Young Male. 3. Female & Nest.
Honey Locust.

Drawn from Nature by J.J.Audubon.F.R.S.F.L.S.

Lith.d Printed & Col.d b, ͏ᵗ Bowen.Phil.

Pl. 220.

Boat-tailed Grackle.

1. Male. 2. Female.

Live Oak.

Drawn from Nature by J.J.Audubon. F.R.S.F.L.S.　　　　Lithᵈ Printed & Colᵈ by J. T. Bowen. Phil.

R.T.

Brewers Black-bird.

Male.

Drawn from Nature by J.J.Audubon F.R.S. F.L.S.   Lith Printed & Col⁴ by J. T. Bowen, Philadᵃ.

Common, or Purple Crow-Blackbird.

1. Male. 2. Female.

Maize or Indian Corn.

Drawn from Nature by J.J. Audubon, F.R.S. F.L.S.   Lith. Printed & Col.d by J.T. Bowen, Philad.

Rusty Crow-Blackbird.

1. Male. 2. Female. 3. Young.
Black Haw.

Drawn from Nature by J. J. Audubon F.R.S.F.L.S.   Lith.ᵈ Printed & Col.ᵈ by J. T. Bowen Philad.

R.T.

Meadow Starling or Meadow Lark.
1. *Males.* 2. *Female and Nest.*
Yellow flowered Gerardia.

Drawn from Nature by J.J.Audubon,F.R.S.F.L.S.   Lithd Printed & Cold by J. T. Bowen, Philada.

W.E.H.

Missouri Meadow Lark.

Male

Drawn from Nature by J.J.Audubon, F.R.S.F.L.S.   Lith. Printed & Col.ᵈ by J.T.Bowen, Philadᵃ.

Common American Crow

Male.

Black Walnut

Drawn from Nature by J. J. Audubon. F.R.S.F.L.S   Lith.ᵈ Printed & Col.ᵈ by J. T. Bowen. Phil

Fish Crow.

1 Male. 2 Female.

Honey Locust.

Drawn from Nature by J. J. Audubon F.R.S.F.L.S.   Lith.d Printed & Col.d by J. T. Bowen Phil.

Raven

Old Male.

Thick-Shell bark Hickory.

Drawn from Nature by J.J. Audubon. F.R.S.F.L.S.   Lithᵈ Printed & Colᵈ by J.T. Bowen. Philad.

Columbia Magpie or Jay.

Males

Drawn from Nature by J. J. Audubon. F.R.S.F.L.S.   Lithd Printed & Cold by J. T. Bowen. Phil.

Common Magpie.

1. Male 2. Female.

Drawn from Nature by J.J.Audubon.F.R.S.F.L.S.   Lith.ᵈ Printed & Col.ᵈ by J.T.Bowen Philad.

Yellow - billed Magpie.

Male.

Plantanus.

Drawn from Nature by J.J.Audubon.F.R.S.F.L.S   Lith⁴.Printed & Col⁴.by J.T Bowen.Philad.

Blue Jay

1. Male. 2 & 3. Female

Trumpet flower. Bignonia radicans.

Drawn from Nature by J.J. Audubon. F.R.S.F.L.S.   Lith.ᵈ Printed & Col.ᵈ by J.T. Bowen. Philad.

Canada Jay

1. Male. 2. Female. 3. Young.
White Oak. Quercus alba.

Drawn from Nature by J.J. Audubon. F.R.S.F.L.S.   Lith.ᵈ Printed & Col.ᵈ by J.T. Bowen. Phil.

Florida Jay
1. Male   2. Female.
Persimontree. Diospyros Virginiana.

Drawn from Nature by J.J.Audubon.F.R.S.F.L.S.   Lithd Printed & Cold by J.T.Bowen.Phil.

R.T.

Stellers Jay

.Male.

Drawn from Nature by J.J. Audubon F.R.S.F.L.S.   Lith.ᵈ Printed & Col.ᵈ by J.T. Bowen. Phil.ᵃ

Ultramarine Jay

Adult Male.

Drawn from Nature by J.J.Audubon.F.R.S.F.L.S.   Lith.ᵈ Printed & Col.ᵈby J.T.Bowen.Phil.

Clarke's Nutcracker.

1. Male. 2. Female.

Drawn from Nature by J.J. Audubon F.R.S. F.L.S

Lith.Printed & Col.d by J.T. Bowen. Philad.

Great American Shrike.

1. Male. 2. Female. 3. Young.

Cratægus Apiifolia.

Drawn from Nature by J.J.Audubon, P.R.S.F.L.S   Lith.d Printed & Col.d by J. T. Bowen. Phil.

R.T.

Loggerhead Shrike

1. Male. 2. Female.

Greenbriar or Round-leaved Smilax. Smilax Rotundifolia

Drawn from Nature by J.J.Audubon. F.R.S.F.L.S.   Lith.ᵈ Printed & Col.ᵈ by J. T. Bowen Philad.

Bartrams Vireo or Greenlet

Male
Ipomea

Drawn from Nature by J.J. Audubon. F.R.S.F.L.S.   Lithd. Printed & Cold by J.T. Bowen. Phil.

Bell's Vireo.
Male.
Rattle-snake Root
Drawn from Nature by J.J.Audubon, F.R.S.F.L.S.   Lith. Printed & Col.ᵈ by J.T.Bowen, Phila.

n.5

Red-eyed Vireo or Greenlet.

Male.
Honey-Locust.

Drawn from Nature by J.J.Audubon.F.R.S.F.L.S.   Lithd Printed & Cold by J.T.Bowen. Phil.

Solitary Vireo or Greenlet.

1 Male. 2 Female.

American Cane. Miegia macrosperma.

Drawn from Nature by J.J. Audubon, F.R.S.F.L.S.   Lithd Printed & Cold by J.T. Bowen Phil.

Warbling Vireo or Greenlet

1 Male. 2. Female.
Swamp Magnolia

Drawn from Nature by J. J. Audubon, F.R.S.F.L.S.   Lith.ᵈ Printed & Colᵈ by J. T. Bowen, Philad.

White-eyed Vireo, or Greenlet.
Male.
Pride of China, or bead tree. Melia Azedarach.

Drawn from Nature by J.J.Audubon. F.R.S.F.L.S.   Lith.d Printed & Col.d by J. T. Bowen. Phil.:

R.T.

Yellow-throated Vireo, or Greenlet.

Male.

Swamp Snowball. *Hydrangea quercifolia.*

Drawn from Nature by J. J. Audubon, F.R.S.F.L.S.   Lith. Printed & Col.d by J. T. Bowen, Philad.

Yellow-breasted Chat.

1. 2. 3. Male 4. Female.
Sweet briar.

Drawn from Nature by J.J. Audubon. F.R.S.F.L.S.   Lith.ᵈ Printed & Col.ᵈ by J.T. Bowen, Phil.

Black throated Wax-wing.
or Bohemian Chatterer.
1. Male. 2. Female.
Canadian Service Tree.

Drawn from Nature by J. J. Audubon. F. R. S. F. L. S.   Lith.ᵈ Printed & Col.ᵈ by J. T. Bowen. Philad.

Cedar bird, or Cedar Wax-wing

1. Male 2. Female.

Red Cedar.

Drawn from Nature by J.J.Audubon.F.R.S.F.L.S   Lithᵈ Printed & Colᵈ by J. T. Bowen Philad.

Brown-headed Nuthatch

1. Male. 2. Female.

Drawn from Nature by J.J.Audubon.F.R.S.F.L.S.   Lith.d Printed & Col.d by J.T.Bowen.Phil.

Californian Nuthatch.

Adults.

Drawn from Nature by J. J. Audubon F.R.S.F.L.S.   Lith.ᵈ Printed & Col.ᵈ by J. T. Bowen Phil.

Pl. 248.

Red-bellied Nuthatch

1. Male 2. Female.

Drawn from Nature by J. J. Audubon, F.R.S.F.L.S.   Lith.ᵈ Printed & Col.ᵈ by J. T. Bowen, Phil.

3.

1.

2.

White-breasted Nuthatch.

1. Male. 2 & 3. Female

Drawn from Nature by J.J.Audubon. F.R.S.F.L.S.

Lith.ᵈ Printed & Col.ᵈ by J. T. Bowen Phil.

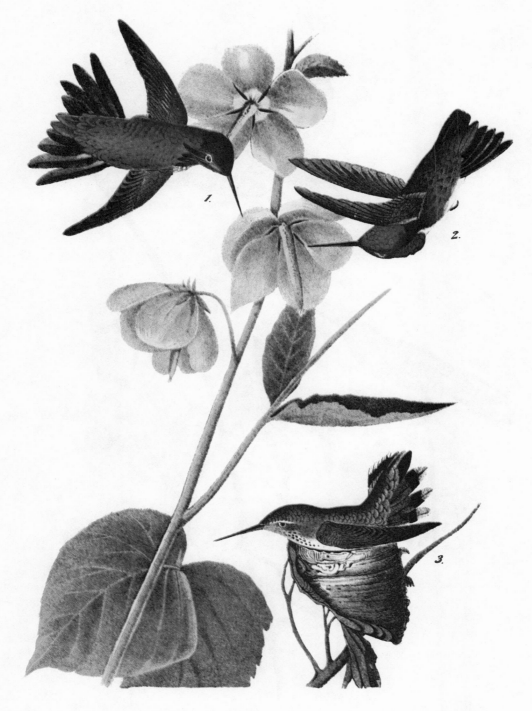

Anna Humming bird.

1. 2. Males. 3 Female.

Hibiscus Virginicus.

Drawn from Nature by J.J.Audubon,FRSFLS.   Lith.ᵈ Printed & Col.ᵈ by J.T. Bowen, Philad.ᵃ

AV.

Mango Humming bird
1. 2. Males. 3. Female
Bignonia grandifolia.

Drawn from Nature by J.J. Audubon. F.R.S.F.L.S.   Lith.d Printed & Col.d by J.T. Bowen. Phil.

Ruby-throated Hummingbird

1. 2. Males. 3. Female. — 4 Young
(Bignonia - radicans)

Drawn from Nature by J.J. Audubon. F.R.S.F.L.S.   Lith.ᵈ Printed & Col.ᵈ by J. T. Bowen. Phil.ᵃ

Ruff-necked Humming bird.

1. 2. Males. 3. Female.

Cleome heptaphylla.

Drawn from Nature by J.J. Audubon, F.R.S.F.L.S.   Lithd Printed & Cold by J.T. Bowen, Phil.

Belted Kingfisher
Alcedo Alcyon.

1. Males 2. Female

Drawn from Nature by J.J. Audubon. F.R.S.F.L.S.   Lith⁴ Printed & Col⁴ by J.T. Bowen, Phil.

A.V.

Arctic three-toed Woodpecker.

1. 2. Males. 3. Female.

Drawn from Nature by J.J.Audubon. F.R.S.F.L.S.   Lith.ᵈPrinted & Col.ᵈby J.T.Bowen. Phil.

A.V.

Audubons' Woodpecker.

Male.

Drawn from Nature by J.J. Audubon F.R.S.F.L.S.   Lith.ᵈ Printed & Col.ᵈ by J.T. Bowen, Phil.

Banded three-toed Woodpecker.

1. Male 2. Female.

Drawn from Nature by J.J. Audubon. F.R.S.F.L.S.

W.H.

Canadian Woodpecker.

Male.

Drawn from Nature by J.J.Audubon.F.R.S.F.L.S   Lith.ª.Printed & Col.ª by J.T.Bowen.Phil.

1.

2.

Downy Woodpecker

1 Male. 2 Female

Drawn from Nature by J.J. Audubon F.R.S.F.L.S.   Lith.ª Printed & Col.ª by J.T.Bowen, Phil.

Golden-winged Woodpecker

1. Male. 2. Females.

Drawn from Nature by J.J. Audubon. F.R.S.F.L.S.   Lithᵈ Printed & Colᵈ by J.T. Bowen. Phil.

Hairy Woodpecker.

1. Male 2. Female

Drawn from Nature by J.J Audubon F.R.S.F.LS.   Lithd Printed & Cold by J.T. Bowen Phil.

Harris's Woodpecker

1. Male. 2. Female.

Drawn from Nature by J. J. Audubon. F.R.S.F.L.S.

Lithᵈ Printed & Colᵈ by J. T. Bowen. Phil

Ivory-billed Woodpecker.

1 Male. 2 & 3 Female.

Drawn from Nature by J.J. Audubon. F.R.S.F.L.S.   Lithᵈ Printed & Colᵈ by J.T. Bowen, Phil.

Lewis' Woodpecker.

1. Male 2. Female

Drawn from Nature by J.J.Audubon.F.R.S.F.L.S.   Lith.ᵈ Printed & Col.ᵈ by J.T.Bowen Phil.

Maria's Woodpecker.

1. Male. 2. Female.

Drawn from Nature by J.J.Audubon,F.R.S.F.L.S.   Lith.ᵈ Printed & Col.ᵈ by J.T.Bowen,Phil.

W.E.H.

Missouri Red-moustached Woodpecker

Male

Drawn from Nature by J.J.Audubon,F.R.S.F.LS

Lith Printed & Col.ᵈ by J.T.Bowen,Philad.ᵃ

Phillips' Woodpecker.

Males.

Drawn from Nature by J.J.Audubon.F.R.S.F.L.S.   Lith.d Printed & Col.d by J.T. Bowen Phil.

Pileated Woodpecker
1. Adult Male. 2. Adult Female. 3 and 4. Young Males.
Raccoon Grape.

Drawn from Nature by J.J.Audubon. F.R.S.F.L.S.　　　　　　　Lith.ᵈ Printed & Col.ᵈ by J.T.Bowen. Phil.

Red-bellied Woodpecker.

1. Male. 2. Female.

Drawn from Nature by J. J. Audubon. F.R.S.F.L.S.   Lith.ᵈ Printed & Col.ᵈ by J. T. Bowen. Phil.

Red-breasted Woodpecker.

1. Male. 2. Female.

Drawn from Nature by J.J.Audubon.F.R.S.F.L.S.   Lithᵈ.Printed & Colᵈ.by J.T.Bowen.Phil.

Red-cockaded Woodpecker.

1. 2. Males 3. Female.

Drawn from Nature by J.J. Audubon F.R.S.F.L.S.   Lith.ᵈ Printed & Col.ᵈ by J.T. Bowen. Phil.

Red-headed Woodpecker.

1. Male. 2. Female. 3 Young.

Drawn from Nature by J.J.Audubon, F.R.S.F.L.S.   Lithᵈ Printed & Colᵈ by J. T. Bowen, Philadᵈ

Red-shafted Woodpecker.

1. Male. 2. Female.

Drawn from Nature by J.J.Audubon.F.R.S.F.L.S.   Lith.& Printed & Col.ᵈ by J.T.Bowen.Phil.

1.

2.

Yellow-bellied Woodpecker.

1. Male. 2. Female.
Prunus Caroliniana.

Drawn from Nature by J.J.Audubon. FRS ELS   Lith.ᵈ Printed & Col.ᵈ by J.T.Bowen Phil.

Pl. 276

N°. 56

Black-billed Cuckoo.
1.Male 2.Female.
Magnolia grandiflora.

Drawn from Nature by J.J.Audubon.F.R.S.F.L.S.

Lith.Printed & Col.d by J.T.Bowen.Phil.

W.H.

Mangrove Cuckoo.

Male.
Seven years apple.

Drawn from Nature by J.J. Audubon, F.R.S. F.L.S.   Lith.ᵈ Printed & Col.ᵈ by J.T. Bowen Phil.

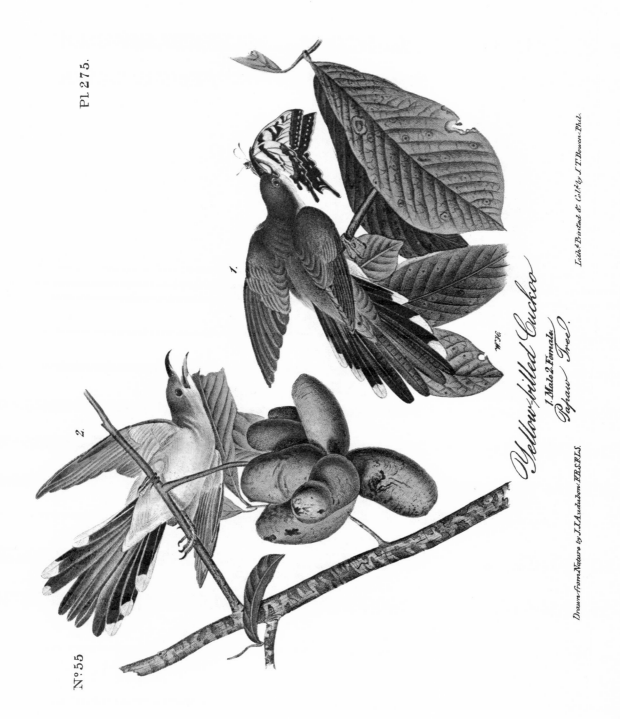

Pl. 275.

N.º 55

Yellow-billed Cuckoo
1. Male 2. Female.
Papaw Tree.

Drawn from Nature by J.J.Audubon, F.R.S.F.L.S.

Lith.ᵈ Printed & Col.ᵈ by J.T.Bowen. Phil.ᵃ

Carolina Parrot or Parrakeet

1. 2. Males . 3. Female . 4. Young.
Cockle bur.

Drawn from Nature by J.J. Audubon FRSFLS.   Lith.d Printed & Col.d by J.T. Bowen. Phil.

2.

1.

A.V.

Band-tailed Dove or Pigeon.

1. Male. 2. Female.

Cornus nuttalli

Drawn from Nature by J.J. Audubon, F.R.S. F.L.S.

Lith. Printed & Col.d by J.T. Bowen Phil.

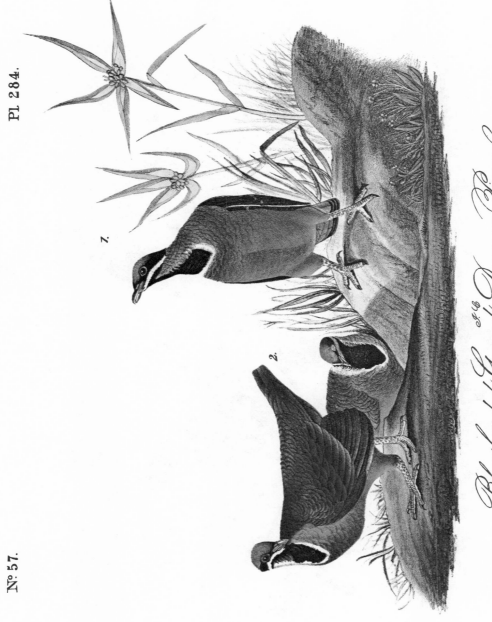

No 57.

Pl 284.

Blue-headed Ground Dove or Pigeon.
1. Male. 2. Females.

Drawn from Nature by J.J.Audubon.F.R.S.F.L.S.

Lith.Printed.&Col.by J.T.Bowen. Phil.

Ground Dove.
1. & 2. Males. 3. Female. 4. Young
Wild Orange.

Drawn from Nature by J.J. Audubon.F.R.S.F.L.S.   Lith.ᵈ Printed & Col.ᵈ by J. T. Bowen. Phil.

N°. 57.

Pl. 282.

1.

2.

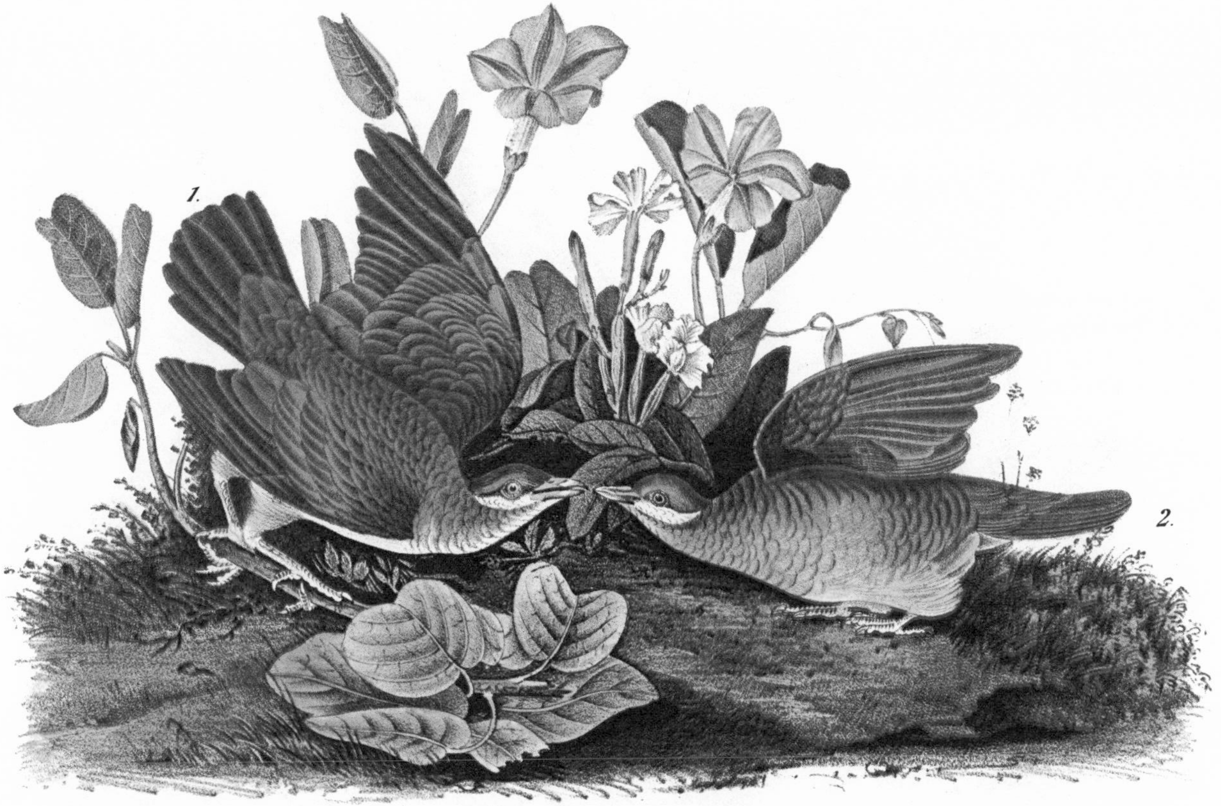

Key-West Dove

1. Male. 2. Female.

Drawn from Nature by J. J. Audubon, F.R.S. F.L.S.

Lith.d Printed & Col.d by J. T. Bowen, Philad.

N.T.

The Texan Turtle Dove.

Male.

Drawn from Nature by J.J.Audubon, F.R.S. F.L.S   Lith Printed & Col.ᵈ by J.T.Bowen, Philadᵃ

.A.V.

White-headed Dove, or Pigeon

1. Male. 2. Female.

Cordia sebestina.

Drawn from Nature by J.J.Audubon.F.R.S.F.L.S.   Lith.ᵈ Printed & Col.ᵈ by J. T. Bowen. Phil.

Zenaida Dove.

1. Male. 2. Female.

Anona.

Drawn from Nature by J.J. Audubon. F.R.S.F.L.S.   Lith & Printed & Col.d by J. T. Bowen. Philad.

2.

1.

Passenger Pigeon
1. Male 2. Female.

Drawn from Nature by J.J. Audubon F.R.S.F.L.S.   Lith⁴ Printed & Col⁴ by J.T. Bowen Phil⁴

Carolina Turtle Dove.

1. Males 2. Females.

White flowered Stuartia. Stuartia Malacodendron.

Drawn from Nature by J. J. Audubon, F.R.S.F.L.S.

Lithᵈ Printedᵈ & Colᵈ by J. T. Bowen, Philadᵃ

Pl. 288.

Wild Turkey.

Female & Young.

Drawn from Nature by J.J.Audubon,F.R.S.F.L.S.

Lith.ᵈPrinted & Col.ᵈ by J. T. Bowen, Phil.ᵈᵃ

J.C.
Wild Turkey
Male.

Drawn from Nature by J.J.Audubon, FRS.FLS.   Lith.ᵈ Printed & Col.ᵈ by J.T.Bowen, Phil.

No. 58. Pl. 289.

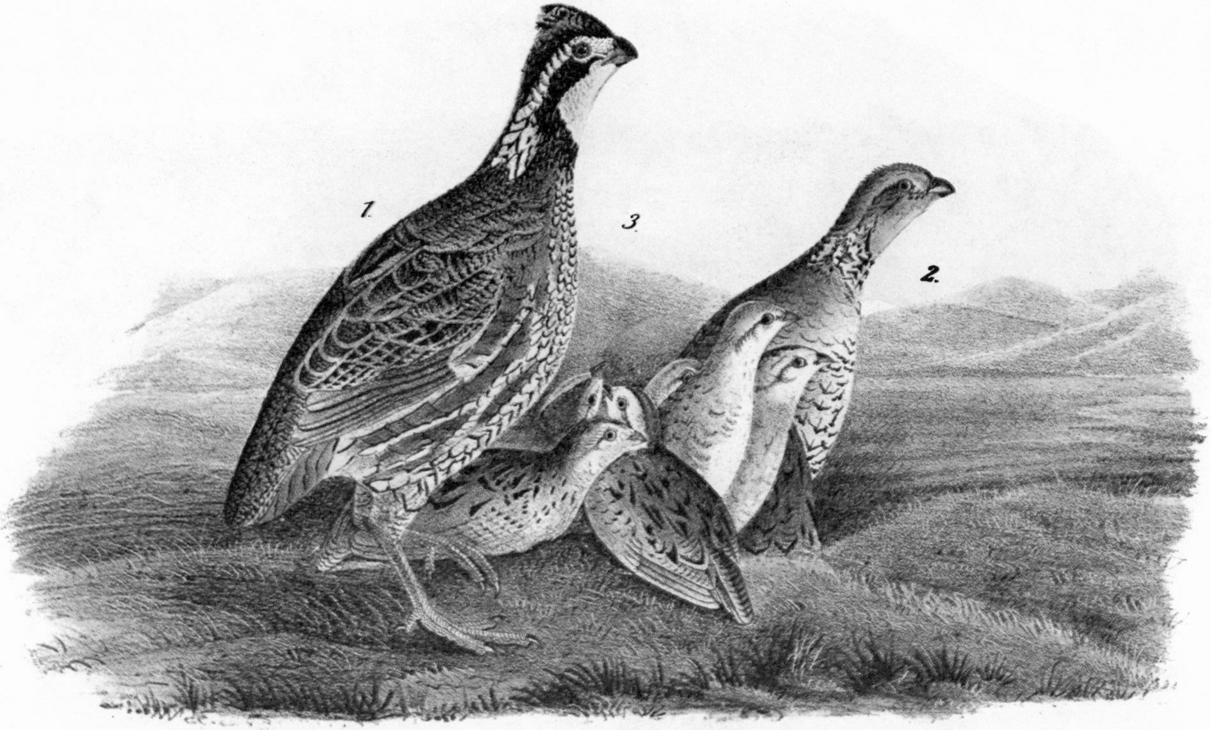

Common American Partridge.

Drawn from Nature by J.J. Audubon, F.R.S.F.L.S.

1. Male. 2. Female. 3. Young.

Lith.d Printed & Col.d by J. T. Bowen, Philad.

N°58. Pl 290.

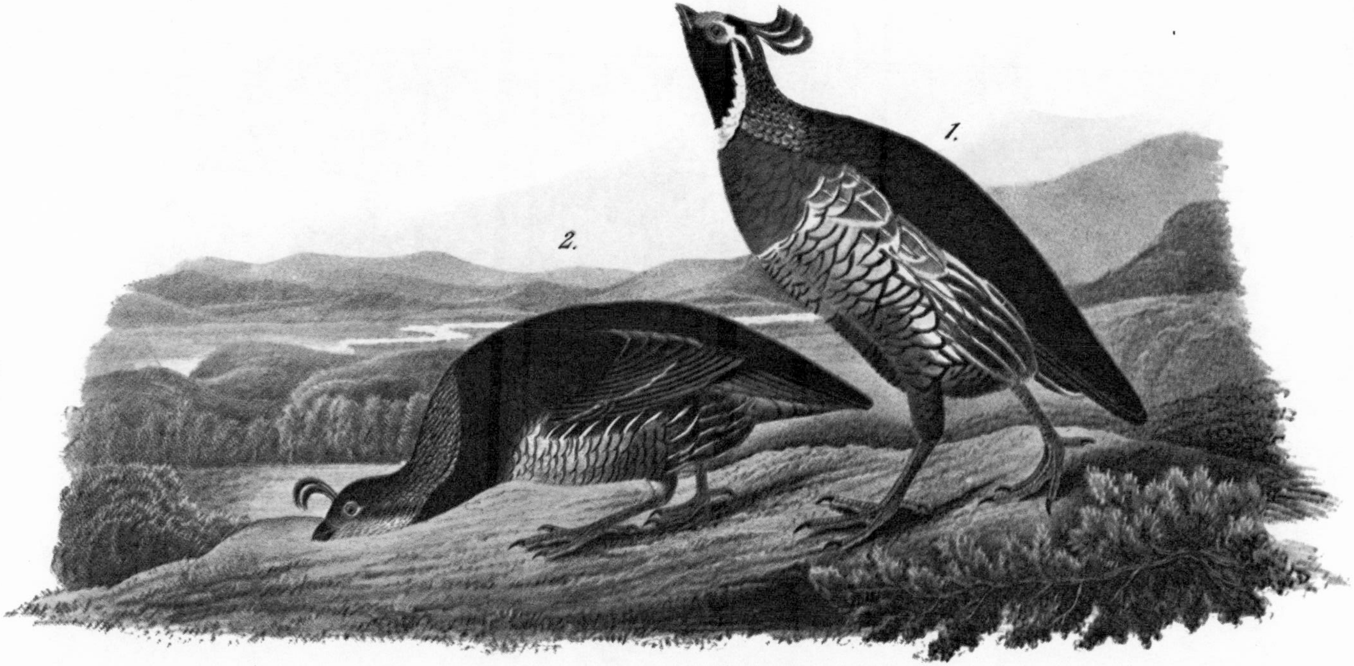

J.C.

Californian Partridge

1. Male. 2. Female.

Drawn from Nature by J.J.Audubon F.R.S.F.L.S.

Lith.d Printed & Col.d by J.T.Bowen Phil.

Pl. 291.

Plumed Partridge.
1. Male. 2. Female.

Drawn from Nature by J.J.Audubon.F.R.S.F.L.S.

Pl 292.

Fig. 2

Welcome Partridge
Young

Drawn from Nature by J.J.Audubon, F.R.S.F.L.S.

Lith?.Printed & Col?.by J.T.Bowen, Phil.

Pl. 294.

Canada Grouse!

1.2. Males. 3. Females.
4. Fulivus pictum. 5. Krophus distortus.

Drawn from Nature by J.J.Audubon.F.R.S.F.L.S

Lith.ᵈ Printed & Col.ᵈ by J.T.Bowen. Phil.

Pl 297.

N° 60.

Drawn from Nature by J.J.Audubon F.R.S.F.L.S

Cock of the Plains.
N°. 76
1. Male 2. Female

Lith Printed & Col.by J.T.Bowen.Phil

N°59.

Dusky Grouse.
1.Male.2.Female

Drawn from Nature by J.J.Audubon.F.R.S.F.L.S

Lith.d Printed & Col.d by J.T.Bowen. Philad.

Pinnated Grouse.

1. 2. Males. 3 Female. Lilium Superbum.

Drawn from Nature by J.J.Audubon.F.R.S.F.L.S.

Lith.Printed & Col.d by J.T.Bowen. Philad.a

Pl. 293.

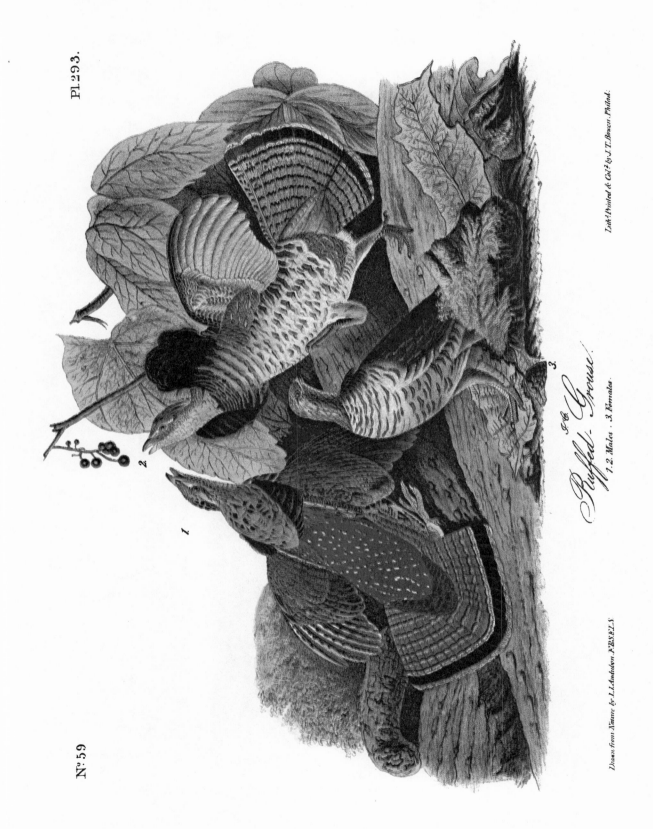

Drawn from Nature by J.J.Audubon. F.R.S.F.L.S.

Ruffed Grouse.
1. 2. Males . 3. Females.

Lith. Printed & Col.d by J.T.Bowen, Philad.

W.H. Sharp-tailed Grouse.
1. Male. 2. Female.

Drawn from Nature by J.J.Audubon, F.R.S.F.L.S

Lith.Printed & Col.by J.T.Bowen, Phil.

Pl. 300.

American Ptarmigan.
Male.

Drawn from Nature by J.J.Audubon.F.R.S.F.L.S.

Lith:Printed & Col:by J.T.Bowen.Phil:

Pl. 301.

2

1

3

Rock Ptarmigan

1. Male, in Winter. 2. Female, Summer Plumage. 3. Young in August.

Drawn from Nature by J.J.Audubon.F.R.S.F.L.S.

Lith.d Printed & Col.d by J.T.Bowen, Philad.

Pl. 302.

N.º 61

White-tailed Ptarmigan
Adult, in Winter Plumage

Drawn from Nature by J.J.Audubon.F.R.S.F.L.S

Lith.ᵈPrinted & Col.ᵈby J.T.Bowen,Philad.

Willow Ptarmigan?
1. Male. 2. Female & young.

Drawn from Nature & by J.J.Audubon. FRSFLS

Lith.d Printed & Cold by J.T.Bowen.Phila.

N.º 61.

Pl 304.

N.º 76.

Common Gallinule!

Adult Male.

Drawn from Nature by J.J. Audubon, F.R.S.F.L.S.

Lith. Printed & Col.d by J. T. Bowen, Philad.ᵃ

Pl. 303.

Drawn from Nature by J.J.Audubon.F.R.S.F.L.S.

Purple Gallinule
Adult Male. Spring Plumage

Lith.ᵈ Printed & Col.ᵈ by J.T.Bowen, Phil.

No. 61.

Pl. 305.

Drawn from Nature by J.J.Audubon. FRS.FLS

American Coot!

Lith.d Printed & Col.d by J.T.Bowen, Philad.a

Pl. 308.

Least Water-Rail.

1. Adult Male. 2. Young.

324

Sora Rail.

1. Male. — 2. Female. 3. Young.

Pl. 307.

Yellow-breasted Rail.
Adult Male in Spring

Drawn from Nature by J.J.Audubon, F.R.S.F.L.S.

Lith.d, Printed & Col.d by J. T. Bowen, Phil.

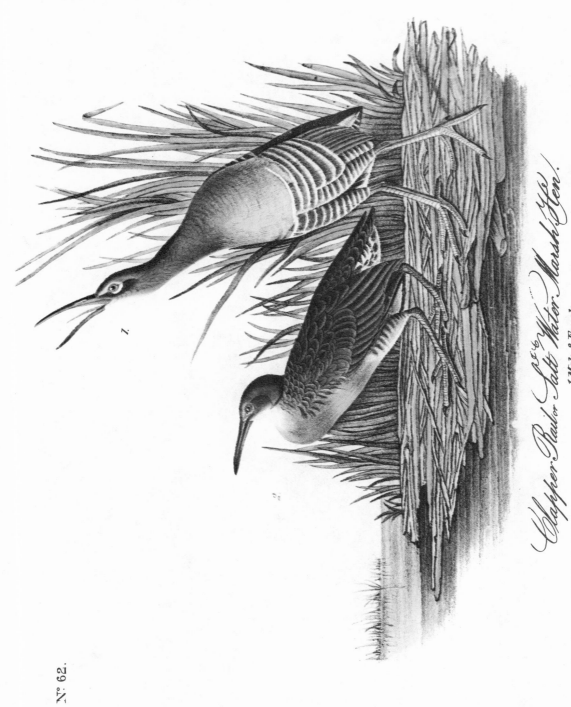

Clapper Rail, or Salt Water Marsh Hen.
1. Male. 2. Female.

RALLUS CREPITANS.

Drawn from Nature by J.J. Audubon, F.R.S.F.L.S.

Lith. Printed & Col.d by J.T. Bowen, Phil.

Pl. 309.

Great Red-breasted Rail, or fresh-water Marsh-Hen.

1. Male adult. 2. Young.

Drawn from Nature by J.J. Audubon, F.R.S.E.L.S.

Lith. Printed & Col. by J.T. Bowen, Phil.

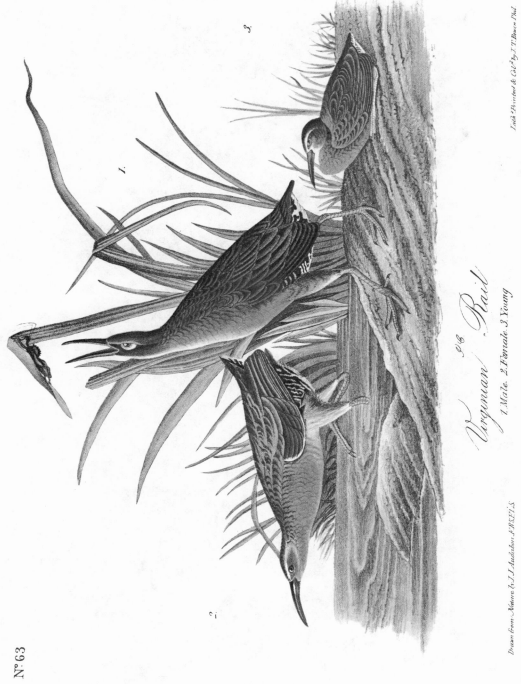

Pl. 311.

Nᵒ 63.

Virginian Rail
1. Male. 2. Female. 3. Young.

Drawn from Nature by J. J. Audubon, F.R.S.E.I.S.

Lith Printed & Colᵈ by J. T. Bowen Phil.

Pl. 312.

Drawn from Nature by J.J. Audubon F.R.S.F.L.S.

Scolopaceous Courlan.

Lith.ᵈ Printed & Col.ᵈ by J.T. Bowen Phil.ᵃ

Whooping Crane.
Male, adult.

Drawn from Nature by J.J.Audubon,F.R.S.E.L.S.   Lithᵈ Printed & Colᵈ by J. T. Bowen, Philadᵃ

Whooping Crane
Young.

Drawn from Nature by J.J.Audubon.F.R.S.F.L.S.   Lith.d Printed & Col.d by J. T. Bowen. Phil.

PL. 316.

N.º 64.

American Golden Plover.

1. Summer Plumage. 2. Winter. 3. Variety in March.

Drawn from Nature by J.J.Audubon. F.R.S.F.L.S.

Lith. Printed & Col.d by J.T.Bowen. Phil.

333

Pl. 320.

2.

1.

American Ring Plover.
1. Adult Male. 2. Young in August.

Drawn from Nature by J.J.Audubon.F.R.S.F.L.S

Lith.d.Printed & Col.d by J.T.Bowen.Phil.

Pl. 315.

Black-bellied Plover.
1. Male. 2. Young in Autumn. 3. Nestling.

Drawn from Nature by J.J. Audubon. FRS.FLS

Lith.ᵈ Printed & Col.ᵈ by J. T. Bowen, Phil.

Pl. 317.

No. 64.

2

1

Killdeer Plover.

1. Male. 2. Female.

Drawn from Nature by J.J.Audubon. F.R.S.F.L.S

Lith. & Printed & Col.d by J.T.Bowen, Phil.

Pl. 321.

N°. 65

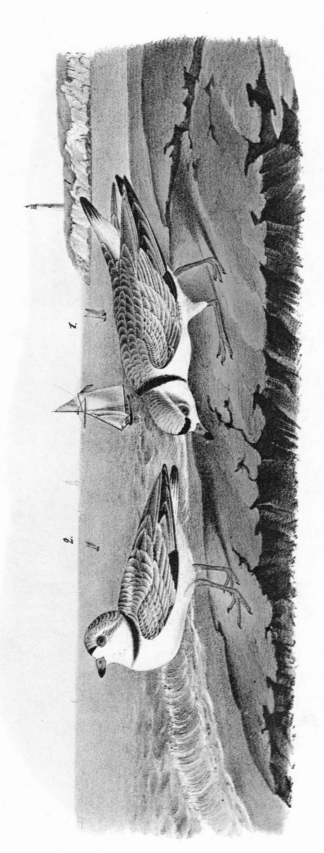

Piping Plover.
1. Male. 2. Female.

Drawn from Nature by J.J.Audubon. F.R.S. F.L.S.

Lith.d Printed & Col.d by J.T. Bowen. Phil.

Pl. 318.

Drawn from Nature by J.J.Audubon.F.R.S.F.L.S

F.

Rocky Mountain Plover.

Female.

Lith.&Printed & Col.d by J.T.Bowen, Phil.

Pl. 319.

Wilson's Plover.

1. Male. 2. Female.

Drawn from Nature by J. J. Audubon. F.R.S.E.L.S.

Lith.ª Printed & Col.ª by J. T. Bowen, Phil.ª

No. 65.

Pl. 322.

Townsend's Surf Bird.
Female.

Drawn from Nature by J. J. Audubon F.R.S.F.L.S.

Lith.d Printed & Col.d by J. T. Bowen Phil.

340

Pl. 323.

Drawn from Nature by J.J.Audubon, F.R.S.F.L.S.

Turnstone. 1. Summer Plumage. 2. Winter.

Lith.d Printed & Col.d by J.T.Bowen, Phil.

N° 65.

Pl 324

Q.T

American Oyster-Catcher

Male.

Drawn from Nature by J.J.Audubon.F.R.S.F.L.S.

Lith Printed & Col.d by J.T.Bowen,Phil.

Pl. 325

Drawn from Nature by J.J.Audubon.F.R.S.F.L.S.

Bachman's Oyster-catcher.
Male.

Lith.Printed & Col.d by J.T.Bowen.Phil.

Pl 326.

Drawn from Nature by J.J.Audubon. F.R.S.F.L.S.

Townsend's Oyster-catcher.
Female.

Lith.d Printed & Col.d by J.T. Bowen. Phil.

Pl. 327.

W.H.

Bartramian Sandpiper.

1. *Male.* 2. *Female.*

Drawn from Nature by J.J.Audubon. F.R.S.F.L.S.

Lith? Printed & Col? by J.T.Bowen. Phil?

Buff-breasted Sand-piper.
1. Male. 2. Female.

Drawn from Nature by J.J. Audubon. F.R.S.F.L.S.

Lith⁴ Printed & Col⁴ by J.T. Bowen. Philad.

Pl.333.

Curlew Sandpiper.
1 Adult Male. 2. Young.

Drawn from Nature by J.J.Audubon. F.R.S.F.L.S.

Lith Printed & Col.d by J.T.Bowen. Phil.

Pl. 337.

Little Sandpiper.

1. Male. Summer plumage. 2. Female.

Drawn from Nature by J.J. Audubon. F.R.S.F.L.S.

Lith.d Printed & Col.d by J. T. Bowen. Phil.

Long-legged Sandpiper.

Drawn from Nature by J.J.Audubon. F.R.S.F.L.S.

Lith.Printed & Cold.by J.T.Bowen.Phil.

Pl. 329.

Pectoral Sandpiper.
1. Male. 2. Female.

Drawn from Nature by J.J. Audubon. FRS FLS

Lith.d Printed & Col.d by J.T. Bowen, Phil.

N.º 66.

Pl. 330.

2.

1.

Purple Sandpiper.

1. Summer. 2. Winter.

Drawn from Nature by J.J.Audubon.F.R.S.F.L.S.

Lith.ᵈ Printed & Col.ᵈ by J.T.Bowen, Phil.

Red-backed Sandpiper

1.Summer Plumage - 2. Winter.

Drawn from Nature by J.J.Audubon.F.R.S.F.L.S.

Lith. Printed & Col.d by J. T. Bowen. Phil.

352

Pl. 328.

W. 331.

Red-breasted Sandpiper.

1. Summer Plumage. 2. Winter.

Drawn from Nature by J.J.Audubon.F.R.S.F.L.S

Lith.d Printed & Cold by J.T Bowen. Phil.

Pl. 338.

Sanderling Sandpiper.
1. Winterplumage. 2. Summer.

Drawn from Nature by J.J.Audubon.F.R.S.F.L.S.   Lith. Printed & Cold by J.T. Bowen. Phil.

N.º 67.

Pl. 335.

Schinz's Sandpiper
1 Male. 2 Female.

Drawn from Nature by J. J. Audubon. F. R. S. F. L. S.

Lith.ᵈ Printed & Col.ᵈ by J. T. Bowen, Phila.

Pl. 336.

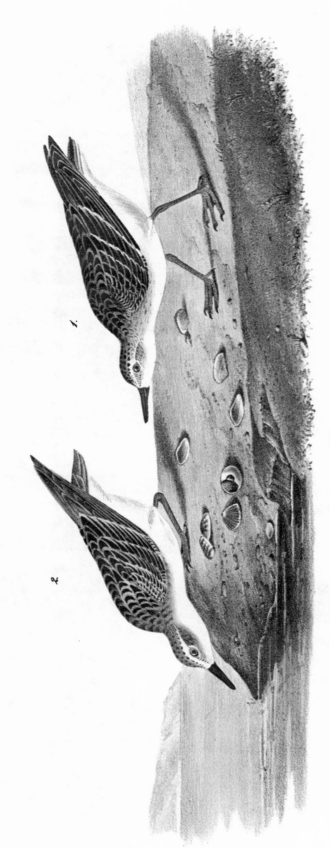

Semipalmated Sandpiper.
1. Summer Plumage. 2. Winter.

Drawn from Nature by J.J. Audubon, F.R.S. F.L.S

Lith.ᵈ Printed & Col.ᵈ by J.T. Bowen, Phila.

Red Phalarope

1. Adult Male. 2. Winter plumage.

Drawn from Nature by J.J.Audubon. F.R.S. F.L.S.

Lith.d Printed & Col.d by J.T.Bowen Philad.

Pl 340.

3.

2.

1.

Hyperborean Phalarope.
1. Male. 2. Female. 3. Young in autumn.

Drawn from Nature by J.J.Audubon.F.R.S.F.L.S.

Lith.d Printed & Col.d by J.T.Bowen,Phil.

W. H.

Wilson's Phalarope.
1, Male, 2 Female.

Pl. 346.

Greenshank
Male.
VIEW OF ST AUGUSTINE & SPANISH FORT FLORIDA.

Drawn from Nature by J.J. Audubon, F.R.S.F.L.S.

Lith.ᵈ Printed & Col.ᵈ by J.T.Bowen, Phila.

Pl. 347.

W.H.

Semipalmated Snipe, Willet, or Stone Curlew.

1. Male Spring Plumage 2. Female in Winter

Drawn from Nature by J.J. Audubon, F.R.S.F.L.S

Lith⁴ Printed & Col⁴ by J.T. Bowen, Phila.

Pl.343.

N°69.

Solitary Sandpiper.
1, Male. 2, Female.

Drawn from Nature by J. J. Audubon, F.R.S. F.L.S.

Lith⁴ Printed & Col⁴ by J. T. Bowen, Phila.

Spotted Sandpiper.
1. Male 2. Female.

Drawn from Nature by J.J. Audubon, F.R.S. F.L.S.

Lith.d Printed & Col.d by J.T. Bowen, Phila.

Pl. 345.

Tell-tale Godwit or Snipe
1. Male. 2. Female.
VIEW OF EAST FLORIDA

Drawn from Nature by J.J. Audubon, F.R.S.F.L.S.

Lith.d Printed & Col.d by J.T. Bowen, Phila.

Pl. 344.

N° 69.

Yellow-Shanks-Snipe.
Male, Summer Plumage.
VIEW IN SOUTH CAROLINA.

Drawn from Nature by J.J.Audubon F.R.S.F.L.S.

Lith.d, Printed & Col.d by J.T.Bowen, Phila.

Pl. 348.

W. H.

Great Marbled Godwit.

1. Male. 2. Female.

Drawn from Nature by J. J. Audubon, F.R.S.F.L.S

Lith*. Printed & Col*. by J. T. Bowen, Philad*.

Pl. 349.

N.º 70.

Hudsonian Godwit.

1. Male. 2. Female Summer Plumage

Drawn from Nature by J. J. Audubon, F.R.S. F.L.S.

Lith.d Printed & Col.d by J. T. Bowen, Phila.

Pl.351.

Red-breasted Snipe.

1, Spring Plumage. 2, Winter

Drawn from Nature by J.J. Audubon, F.R.S.F.L.S.

Lith. Printed & Col.d by J.T.Bowen, Phila.

Pl.350.

Nº70.

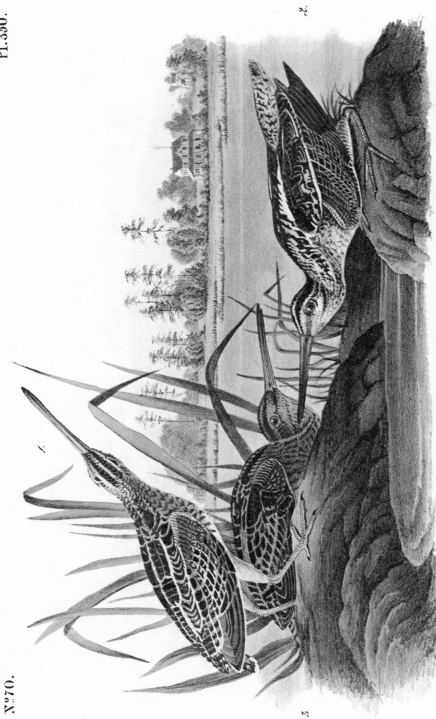

Wilson's Snipe. Common Snipe.
1. Male, 2. & 3. Females.
PLANTATION NEAR CHARLESTON, S.C.

Drawn From Nature by J.J.Audubon, F.R.S. F.L.S.

Lith & Printed & Col.d by J.T.Bowen, Phila.

Pl. 352.

N°71.

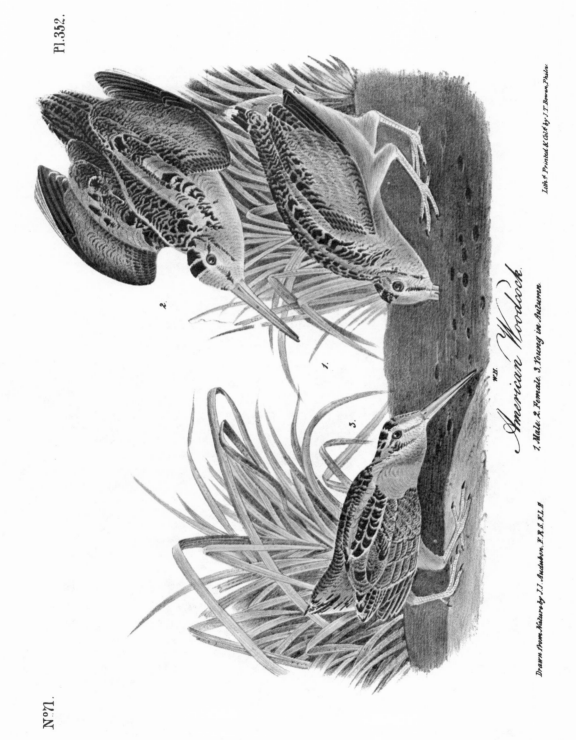

W.E.

American Woodcock.

1. Male. 2. Female. 3. Young in Autumn.

Drawn from Nature by J.J. Audubon. F.R.S. F.L.S

Lith.ᵈ Printed & Col.ᵈ by J.T. Bowen, Philaᵈ

Pl.353.

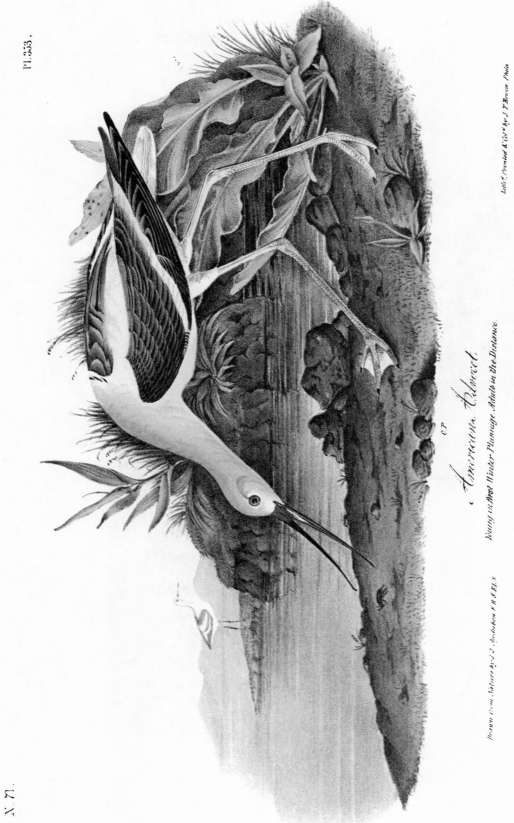

American Avocet.

Young in First Winter Plumage. Adult in the Distance.

Drawn from Nature by J. J. Audubon F R S FLS

Lith d. Printed & Col d. by J. T. Bowen, Phila.

No. 71.

Pl. 354.

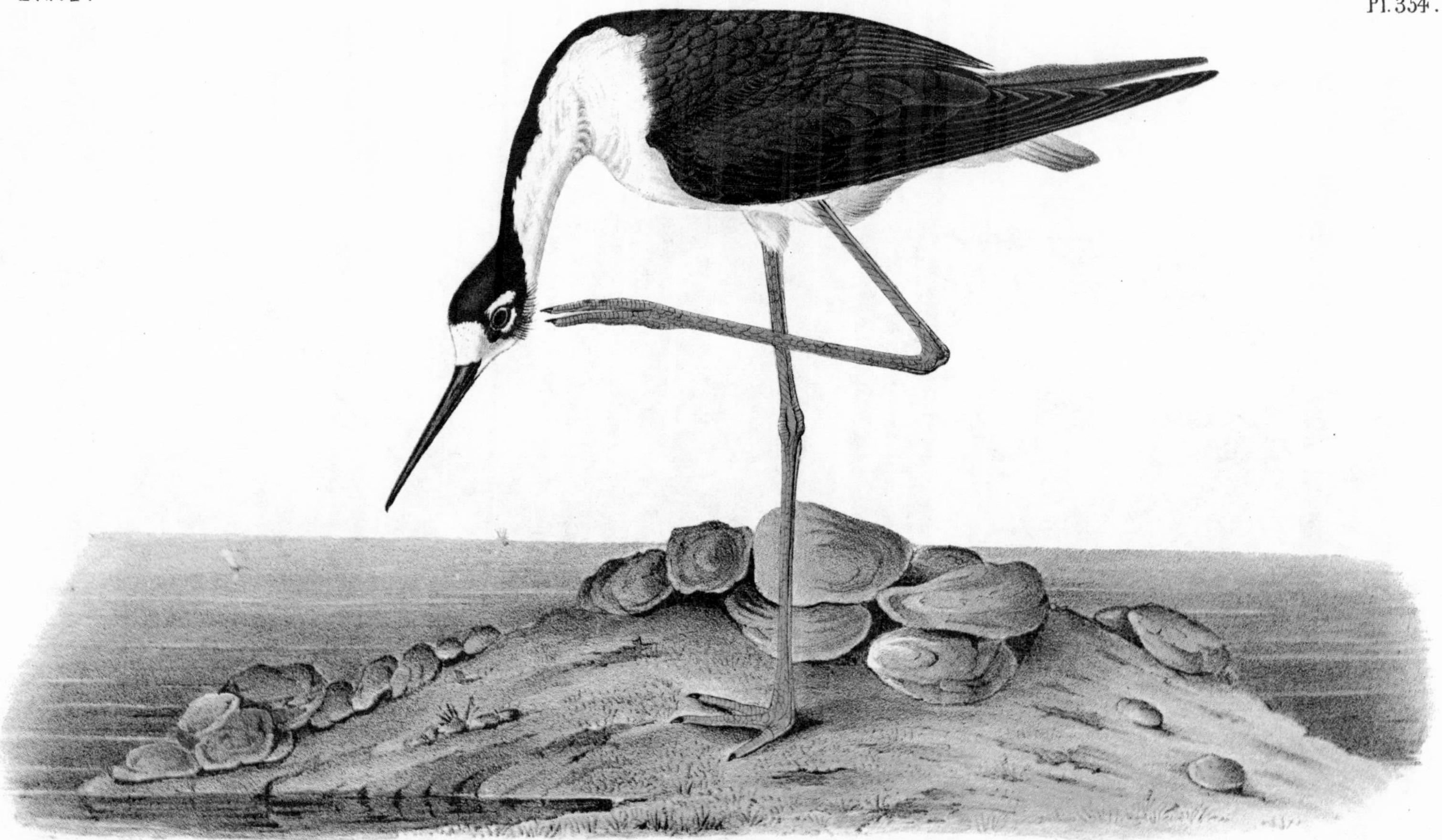

C.P.

Black Necked Stilt

Male.

Drawn from Nature by J. J. Audubon, F.R.S. F.L.S.

Lith.d Printed & Col.d by J. T. Bowen, Phila.

N°.72.

Pl.357.

W.H.

Esquimaux Curlew.
1. Male. 2. Female.

Drawn From Nature by J.J.Audubon,F.R.S. F.L.S.

Lith.d Printed & Col.d by J.T.Bowen, Phila.

373

No. 72.

Pl. 356.

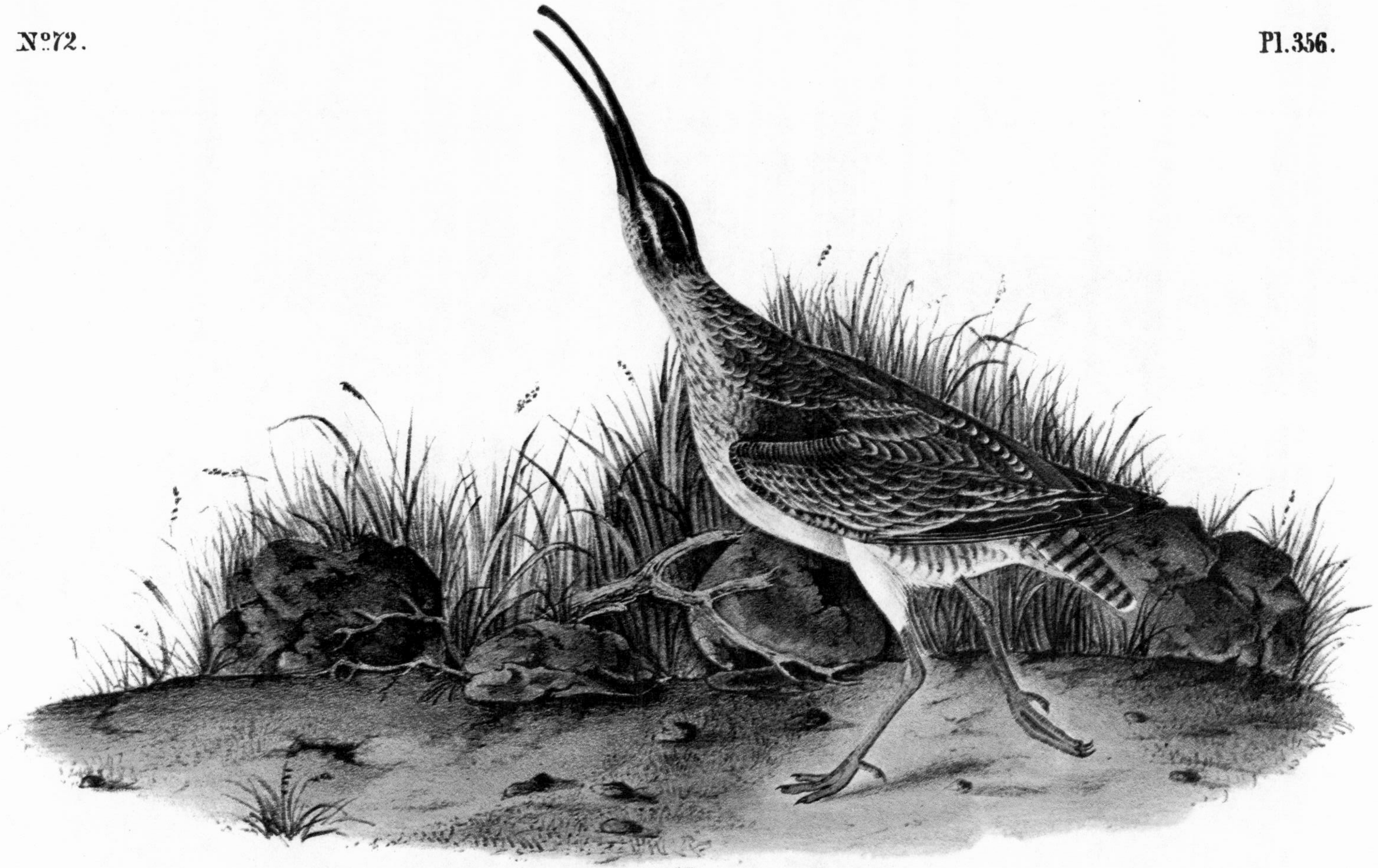

C P

Hudsonian Curlew.

Male

Drawn from Nature by J. J. Audubon F.R.S. F.L.S.

Lith.d Printed & Col.d by J. T. Bowen, Phila.

Pl. 355.

No 71.

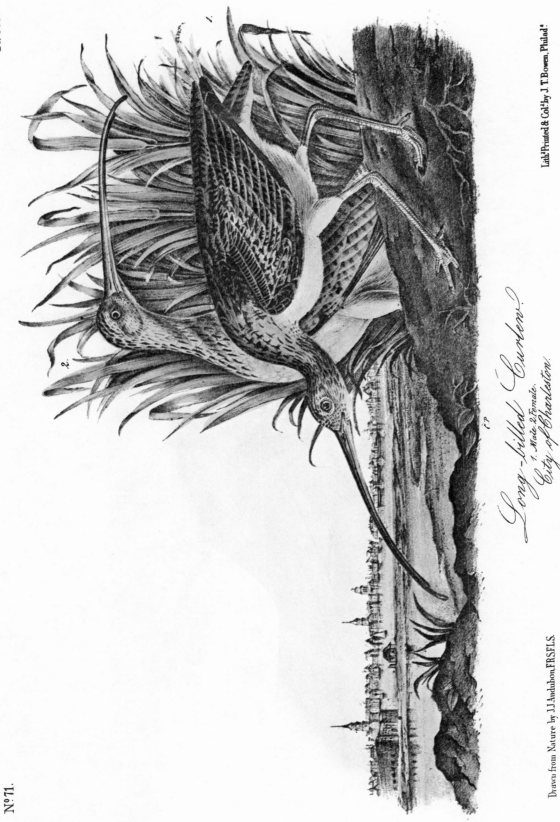

Long-billed Curlew.
1. Male. 2. Female.
City of Charleston.

Drawn from Nature by J.J.Audubon, F.R.S.F.L.S.

Lith.Printed & Col.d by J.T.Bowen, Philad.a

Pl. 358.

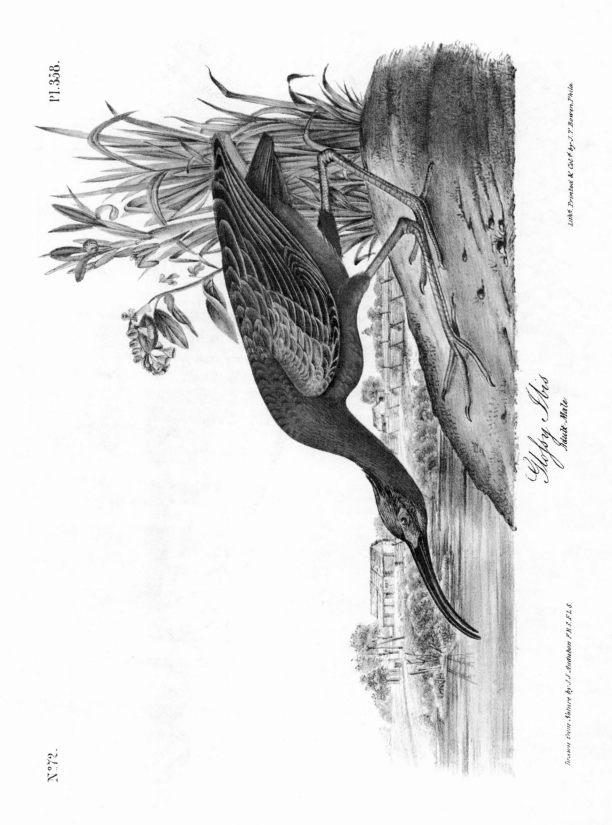

Glossy Ibis.
Adult Male.

Drawn from Nature by J.J. Audubon F.R.S.F.L.S.

Lith. Printed & Col.d by J.T. Bowen, Phila.

Pl. 359.

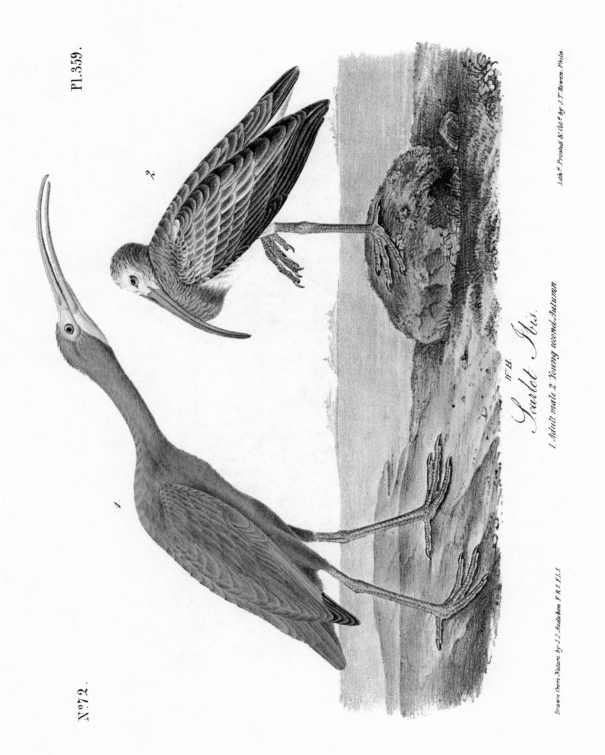

N.ª B.
Scarlet Ibis.
1. Adult male 2. Young second Autumn.

Drawn from Nature by J.J.Audubon. F.R.S.F.L.S

Lith.ª Printed & Col.ª by J.T.Bowen, Phila.

W.B.

White Ibis.

1. Adult, 2. Young in Autumn.

Drawn from Nature by J.J. Audubon, F.R.S. F.L.S.

Lith⁴ Printed & Col⁴ by J.T. Bowen, Phila

W.H.

Wood Ibis.

Male

Drawn from Nature by J.J. Audubon F.R.S.F.L.S.   Lithᵈ Printed & Colᵈ by J.T.Bowen, Philadᵃ

No. 73. Pl. 362.

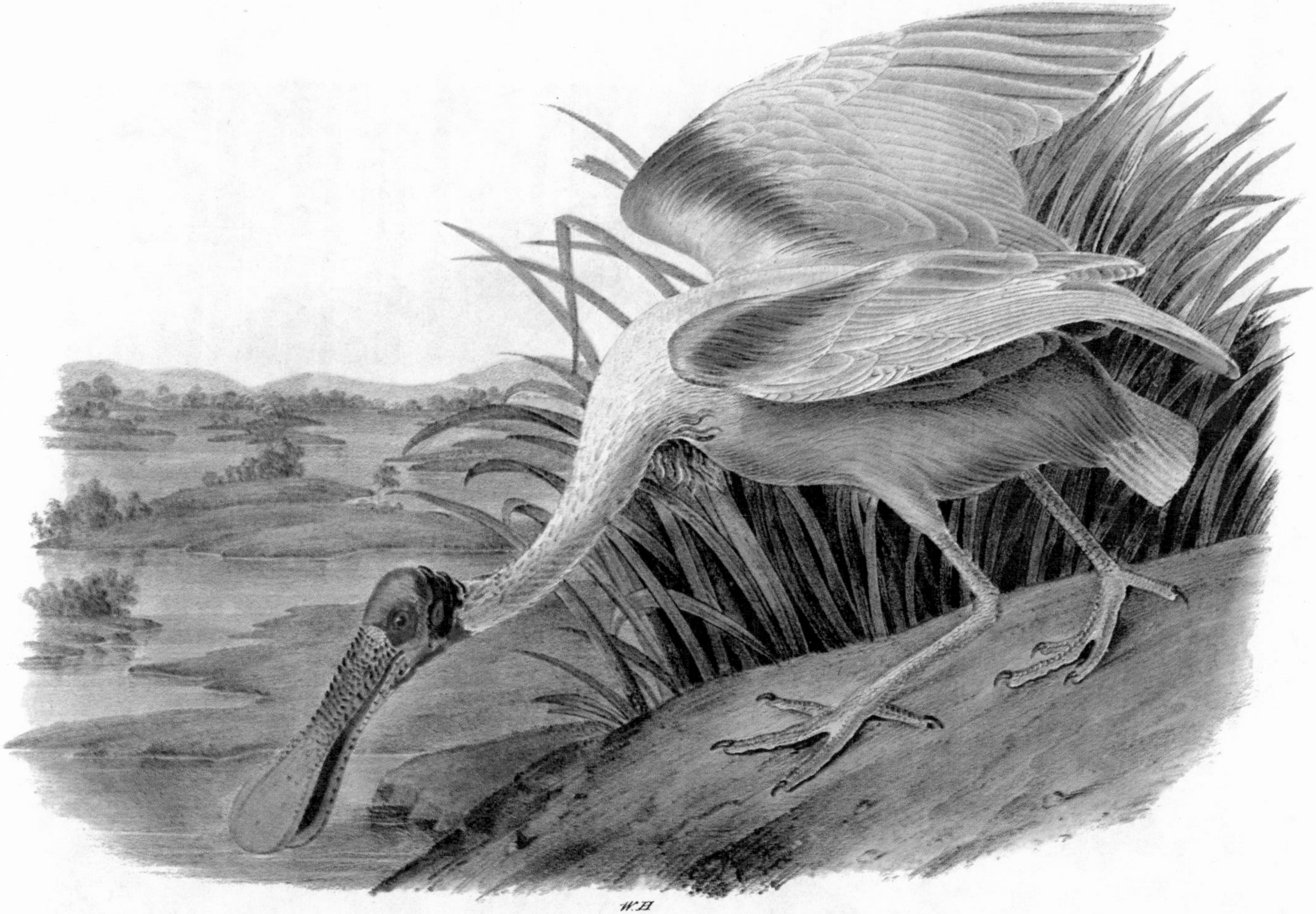

Roseate Spoonbill

Male

Drawn from Nature by J. J. Audubon, F.R.S. F.L.S.

Lith^d. Printed & Col^d. by J. T. Bowen, Philad^a.

Pl. 365.

W.H.

American Bittern

1. *Male. 2. Female*

Drawn from Nature by J. J. Audubon, F.R.S. F.L.S.

Lith.d Printed & Col.d by J. T. Bowen, Phil.a

Pl. 363.

Black-Crowned Night Heron, or Qua Bird.
1. Adult. 2. Young.

Drawn from Nature by J. J. Audubon, F.R.S.F.L.S.

Lith.ᵈ Printed & Col.ᵈ by J. T. Bowen, Phila.

Pl.372.

N.°75.

Blue Heron.

1, Male adult Spring Plumage. 2, Young second Year.

Drawn from Nature by J.J.Audubon, F.R.S.F.L.S

Lith.d Printed & Col.d by J.T.Bowen, Philad.

Pl.370.

N°74.

Great American White Egret.

1. Male, Spring Plumage. 2. Horned Agama Tapayaxin of Hernandez.

Drawn from Nature by J.J Audubon. F.R.S.E.L.S.

Lith Printed & Col.d by J.T. Bowen, Phila.

Great blue Heron.

Male.

Drawn from Nature by J.J.Audubon, F.R.S.F.L.S.

Lith.ᵈ Printed & Col.ᵈ by J. T. Bowen, Philad.ᵈ

Pl.368.

Nº74.

Great White Heron.
Male adult, Spring Plumage.

Drawn from Nature by J.J.Audubon, F.R.S. F.L.S.

Lith Printed & Cold by J.T. Bowen, Philad.ª

386

Pl.367

Green Heron

1. Adult Male. 2. Young in Septr

Drawn from Nature by J.J.Audubon, F.R.S.F.L.S.

Lith Printed & Cold by J.T.Bowen Philad

Pl. 366.

W.H.

Least Bittern.

1, Male. 2, Female. 3, Young.

Drawn from Nature by J.J. Audubon. F.R.S.F.L.S.

Lith⁴ Printed & Col⁴ by J.T.Bowen. Phila.

Pl. 373.

Louisiana Heron?

Male Adult.

No.75.

Drawn from Nature by J.J.Audubon.F.R.S.F.L.S.

Lith.d Printed & Col.d by J.T.Bowen, Philad.a

389

No.75.

Pl.371.

Reddish Egret

1. Adult Full Spring Plumage. 2. Young in Full Spring Plumage two Years old.

Drawn from Nature by J. J. Audubon, F.R.S.F.L.S.

Lith. Printed & Col.ᵈ by J. T. Bowen, Phila.

390

C.P

Snowy Heron
Male.

Drawn from Nature by J.J. Audubon, F.R.S. F.L.S.   Lith. Printed & Col.d by J.T. Bowen Phila.

C.P.

Yellow Crowned Night Heron

1. Adult Male, Spring Plumage 2. Young in October.

Drawn from Nature by J.J. Audubon, F.R.S.F.L.S   Lith.ᵈ Printed & Col.ᵈ by J.T. Bowen, Phila.

American Flamingo.
Adult Male.

Drawn from Nature by J.J. Audubon F.R.S.F.L.S.
Lith. Printed & Col.ᵈ by J. T. Bowen, Phila.

No. 76.

Pl. 378.

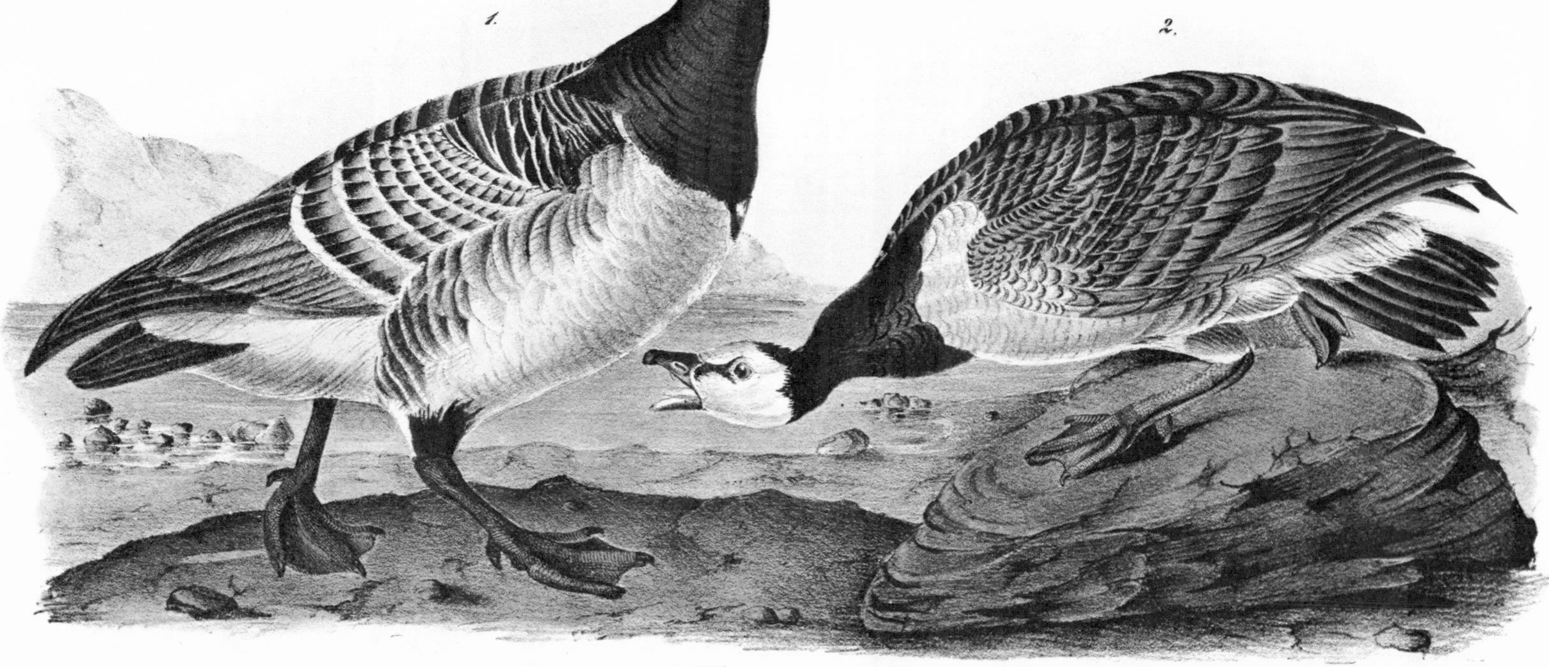

Bernacle Goose

Drawn from Nature by J. J. Audubon F.R.S.F.L.S.

1. Male, 2. Female

Lith. Printed & Col.d by J. T. Bowen, Phila.

Pl.379.

N⁰76.

W.H.
Brant Goose.
1. Male. 2. Female.

Drawn from Nature by J.J.Audubon, F.R.S F.L.S

Lith.ᵈ Printed & Col.ᵈ by J.T.Bowen, Philad.ᵃ

Canada Goose.

1. Male. 2. Female

Drawn from Nature by J. J. Audubon F.R.S.F.L.S

N°76.

Pl.380.

W.H.

White-fronted Goose.
1. Male. 2. Female.

Drawn from Nature by J.J.Audubon, F.R.S. F.L.S.

Lith. Printed & Col.d by J.T.Bowen, Philad.a

C.P.

Hutchins's Goose.

Adult Male.

Drawn from Nature by J.J. Audubon, F.R.S. F.L.S.   Lith⁴ Printed & Col⁴ by J.T. Bowen, Philad⁴

N.º 77.

Pl. 38L.

Snow Goose

1. Adult male. 2. Young Female.

Drawn from Nature by J. J. Audubon, F.R.S. F.L.S.

Lith Printed & Col.d by J. T. Bowen, Phila.

PL 384.

American Swan.

Male.

Drawn from Nature by J.J. Audubon, F.R.S.F.L.S

Lith Printed & Col.d by J.T.Bowen, Phila

Pl. 382.

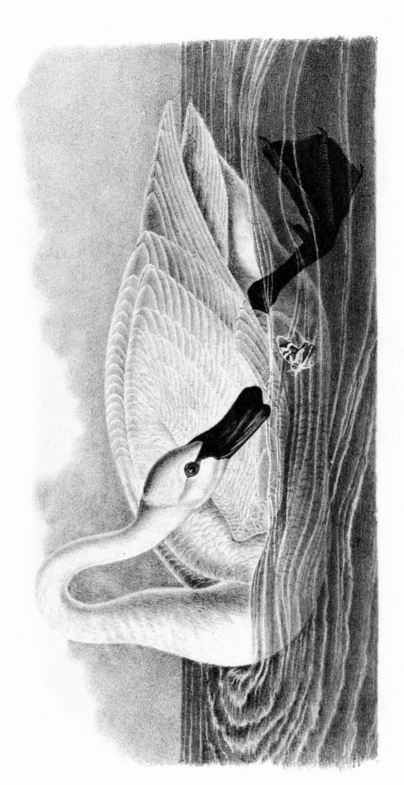

Trumpeter Swan.
Adult.

Drawn from Nature by J.J. Audubon. F.R.S. F.L.S.

Lith. Printed & Col.d by J.T. Bowen, Phila.

Pl. 383.

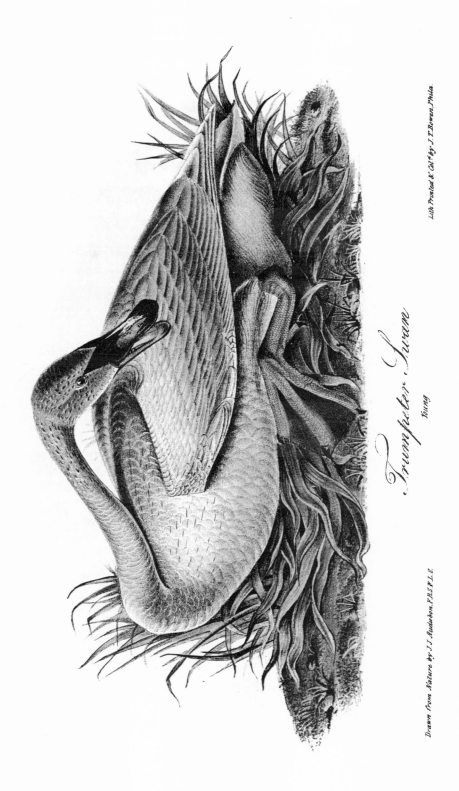

Trumpeter Swan.
Young.

Drawn from Nature by J.J. Audubon, F.R.S.F.L.S.

Lith. Printed & Col.d by J.T. Bowen, Phila.

Pl.389.

American Widgeon
1. Male. 2. Female.

Drawn From Nature by J.J.Audubon,F.R.S.F.L.S

Lith Printed & Col.d by J.T.Bowen,Phila.

Pl.392.

Drawn from Nature by J.J. Audubon, F.R.S. F.L.S.

American Green-winged Teal.
1. Male, 2. Female.

Lith. Printed & Col.ᵈ by J.T. Bowen, Phila.

Drawn from Nature by J.J.Audubon.F.R.S.F.L.S.

Blue-winged Teale

1. Male. 2. Female.

Lithᵈ Printed & Colᵈ by J. T. Bowen, Philadᵃ.

Pl. 387.

R.T.

Brewers Duck.

Male.

Drawn from Nature by J. J. Audubon. F. R. S. F. L. S.

Lith Printed & Col.d by J. T. Bowen. Phila.

Pl. 386.

Dusky Duck.
1. Male 2. Female

Drawn from Nature by J. J. Audubon F.R.S. F.L.S.

Lith. Printed & Col.ª by J.T. Bowen, Phila.

Pl.388.

Gadwall Duck.
1. Male 2. Female

Drawn from Nature by J. J. Audubon, F.R.S.F.L.S.

Lith Printed & Col.d by J.T.Bowen, Phila.

PL.385.

Nº 77.

Mallard

1, 2, Males. 3, 4, Females.

Drawn from Nature by J. J. Audubon, F.R.S.F.L.S.

Lith⁴. Printed & Col⁴ by J. T. Bowen, Philad⁴.

Pl. 390

C.P.

Pintail Duck.

1. Male. 2. Female.

Drawn from Nature by J.J.Audubon, F.R.S.F.L.S.

Lith.ᵈ Printed & Col.ᵈ by J.T.Bowen, Philad.ᵃ

Pl. 394

Drawn from Nature by J.J.Audubon.FRSFLS.

Shoveller Duck

1 Male 2 Female.

Lith.Printed & Col.d by J.T.Bowen.Phil.ad:

C.P.

Wood Duck. Summer Duck.
1. Male. 2. Female.

Drawn from Nature by J.J. Audubon, F.R.S. F.L.S.   Lith. Printed & Colᵈ by J.T. Bowen, Phila.

Pl. 403.

W.H.

American Scoter Duck.
1. Male. 2. Female.

Drawn from Nature by J.J. Audubon. F.R.S. F.L.S.

Lith. Printed & Col.ᵈ by J.T. Bowen, Philad.ᵃ

Pl. 402.

Black or Surf Duck.
1. Male 2. Female.

Pl. 108

Buffel-headed Duck
1. Male. 2. Female.

Drawn from Nature by J.J. Audubon, F.R.S.F.L.S

Lith. Printed & Col. by J.T. Bowen, Phila

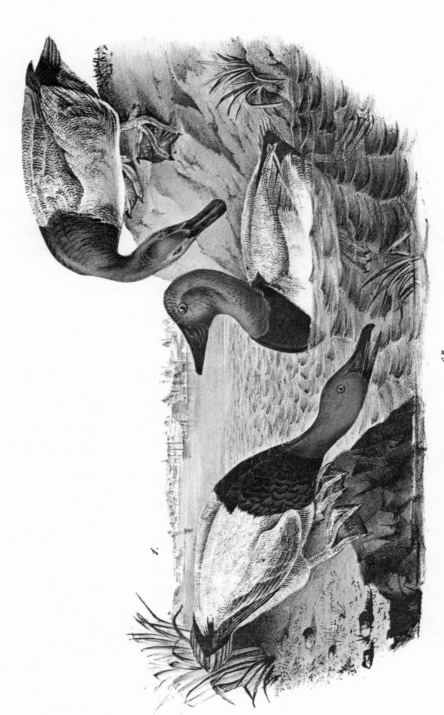

Canvass Back Duck
1 Male 2 Female
VIEW OF BALTIMORE, MARYLAND

Drawn from Nature by J.J.Audubon, F.R.S.F.L.S.

Lith.ᵈ Printed & Col.ᵈ by J.T. Bowen, Philad.ᵃ

416

Pl. 498.

N°. 100.

Common Scaup Duck.
1, Male. 2, Female.

Drawn from Nature by J.J. Audubon, F.R.S. F.L.S

Lith. Printed & Col.^d by J.T. Bowen, Philad.^a

No. 81. Pl. 405.

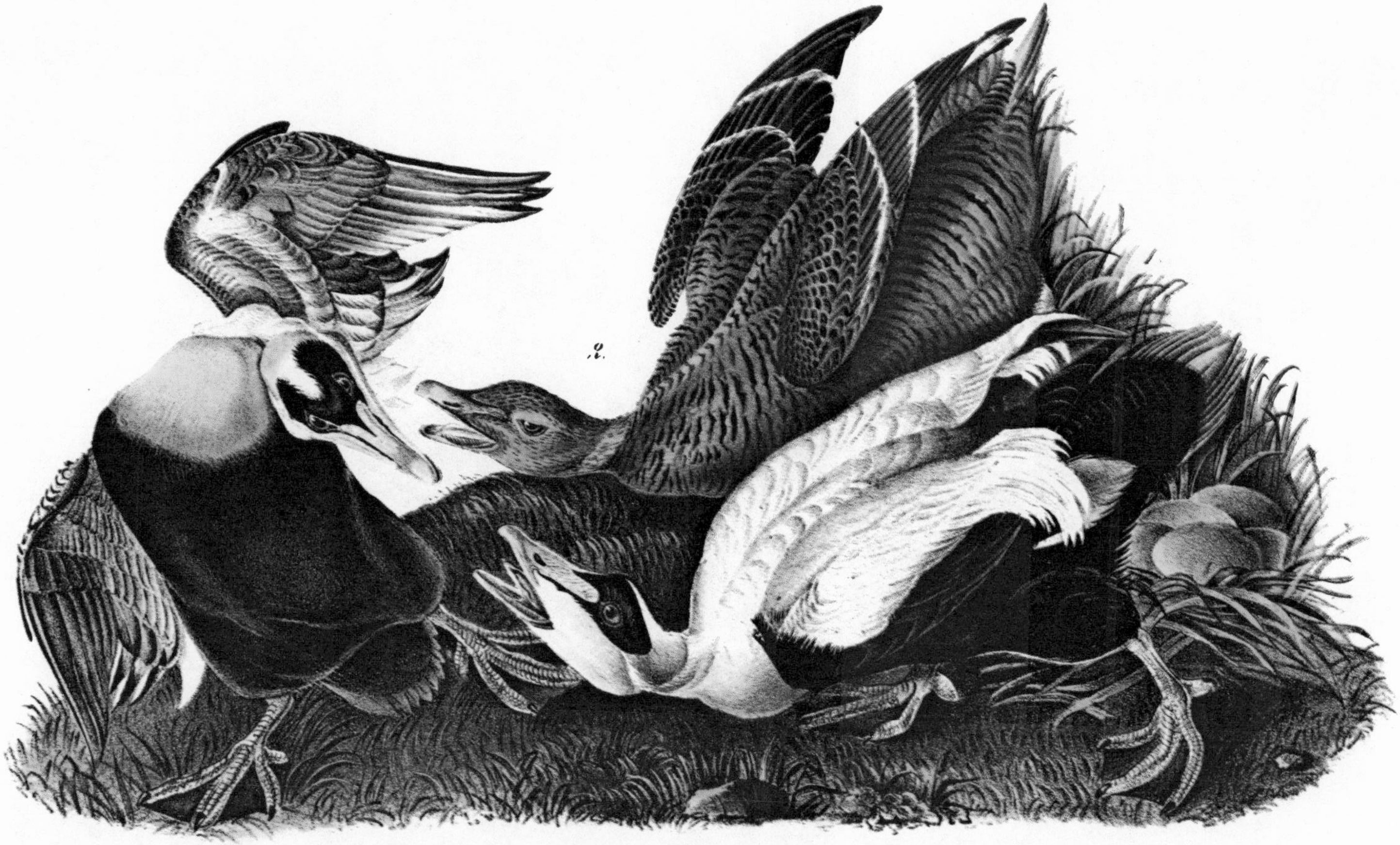

Eider Duck. C.P.

1, Male. 2, Female.

Drawn from Nature by J. J. Audubon F.R.S. F.L.S.

Lith. Printed & Col.d by J. T. Bowen, Phila.

Pl. 406.

2

WH.

1

Golden Eye Duck.
1. Male. 2. Female.

Drawn from Nature by J.J. Audubon. F.R.S.F.L.S.

Lith. Printed & Col.ᵈ by J.T. Bowen, Philad.ᵃ

Pl. 109.

N°. 2

Harlequin Duck
1, old Male, 2, Female, 3, young Male.

Drawn from Nature by J.J. Audubon, F.R.S.F.L.S.

Lith. Printed & Cold by J.T. Bowen, Philad.ª

Pl. 404.

C.P.
King Duck.
1. Male. 2. Female.

Drawn from Nature by J.J. Audubon, F.R.S. F.L.S.

Lith. Printed & Col.ᵈ by J. T. Bowen, Phila.

Pl. 410

Long-tailed Duck.

1. Male, Summer Plumage, 2. Male in Winter. 3. Female and Young.

Drawn from Nature by J. J. Audubon, F. R. S. F. L. s

Lith Printed & Col.d by J. T. Bowen, Philad.a

Pl. 400.

Pied Duck
1. Male 2. Female

Drawn from Nature by J.J. Audubon. F.R.S.F.L.S

Lith. Printed & Col.d by J.T. Bowen. Phila.

Pl. 396

Red-breasted Duck.

W. H.

1. Male. 2. Female.

Drawn from Nature by J.J.Audubon.F.R.S.F.L.S.

Lith^d Printed & Col^d by J.T.Bowen, Philad^a

Pl. 398.

Ring-necked Duck.
1. Male. 2. Female.

R.T.

Drawn from Nature by J.J. Audubon, F.R.S. F.L.S.

Lith. Printed & Col.d by J.T. Bowen, Philad.a

425

Pl. 399.

N° 80.

W.H.

Ruddy Duck

1. Male. 2. Female. 3. Young.

Drawn from Nature by J. J. Audubon, F.R.S. F.L.S.

Lith. Printed & Col.d by J. T. Bowen, Philad.a

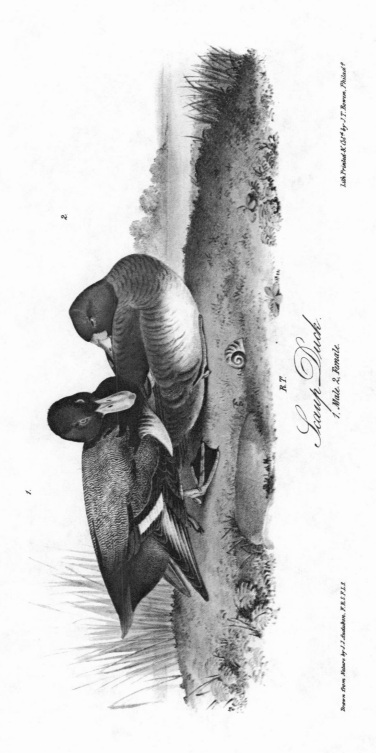

R.T.

Scaup Duck.
1. Male. 2. Female.

Drawn from Nature by J.J. Audubon. F.R.S F.L.S

Lith Printed & Col.d by J.T. Bowen, Philad.a

Pl. 401.

Velvet Duck.
1. Male. 2. Female.

Drawn from Nature by J.J. Audubon, F.R.S. F.L.S.

Lith Printed & Cold by J.T. Bowen, Phila.

428

No. 82. Pl. 407.

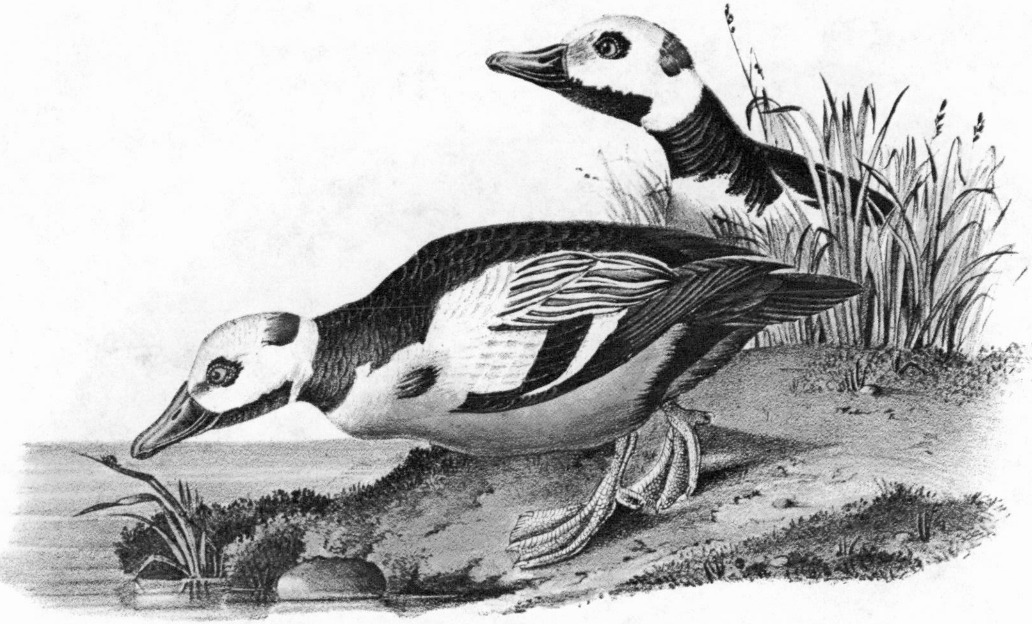

C.P.

Western Duck,

Males

Drawn from Nature by J. J. Audubon, F.R.S.F.L.S. Lith. Printed & Col.d by J. T. Bowen, Philad.a

Buff breasted Merganter. Goosander.
1. Male. 2. Female.

Drawn from Nature by J.J. Audubon, F.R.S. F.L.S.

Lith. Printed & Col.d by J.T. Bowen, Philad.a

Pl. 413.

N°. 83.

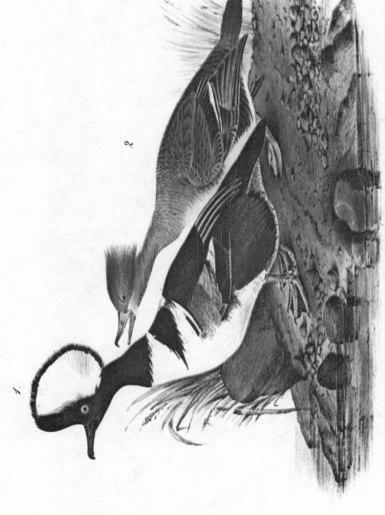

Hooded Merganser.
1, Male. 2, Female.

Drawn from Nature by J.J. Audubon. F.R.S. F.L.S.

Lith. Printed & Col.ᵈ by J.T. Bowen Philad.ᵃ

Pl. 412.

Red-breasted Merganser.

1. Male. 2. Female.

Drawn from Nature by J.J.Audubon, F.R.S.Fl.S.

Lith. Printed & Col.d by J.T.Bowen, Philad.a

W.H.   2

White Merganser Snow White Nun

1. Male. 2. Female.

Drawn from Nature by J.J. Audubon F.R.S. F.L.S.   Lith. Printed & Cold by J.T. Bowen, Philad.ª

Pl.415.

Common Cormorant

1. Male. 2. Female. 3. Young

Drawn from Nature by J.J.Audubon, F.R.S.F.L.S.

Lith. Printed & Col.^d by J.T.Bowen, Philad.^a

Double-crested Cormorant.

Male.

Drawn from Nature by J J Audubon. P R S F L S   Lith. Printed & Col.d by J.T Bowen. Philad.a

Pl. 417.

W.H.

Florida Cormorant.

Male.

Drawn from Nature by J.J. Audubon. F.R.S. F.L.S.

Lith Printed & Cold by J. T. Bowen, Phila.

W. H.

Townsend's Cormorant
Male.

Drawn from Nature by J. J. Audubon, F. R. S. F. L. S.   Lith. Printed & Col.ᵈ by J. T. Bowen, Phila.

C.P.

Violet green Cormorant
Female in Winter

Drawn from Nature by J.J. Audubon, F.R.S.F.L.S.   Lith Printed & Colᵈ by J.T.Bowen, Philadᵃ

American Anhinga Snake Bird
1. Male 2. Female

Drawn from Nature by J.J. Audubon FRSFLS   Lith Printed & Col.d by J.T. Bowen Phila

Frigate Pelican. Man of War Bird.
Male.
Drawn from Nature by J. J. Audubon F. R. S. F. L. S.   Lith Printed & Col'd by J.T. Bowen Phila.

American White Pelican

Male.

Drawn from Nature by J.J.Audubon, F.R.S.F.L.S.   Lithd Printed & Cold by J. T. Bowen, Philadª

Brown Pelican.

Adult Male

Drawn from Nature by J.J.Audubon, F.R.S.F.L.S.   Lith Printed & Col.d by J.T. Bowen, Philadelphia

Pl. 424.

Brown Pelican.
Young first Winter.

Drawn from Nature & on Stone by J. J. Audubon, F.R.S.F.L.S

Lith Printed & Col.d by J.T. Bowen, Philad.a

443

C.P.

Booby Gannet.

Male.

Drawn from Nature by J.J.Audubon, F.R.S.F.L.S Lith. Printed & Col? by J.T.Bowen, Philad?

Pl. 425.

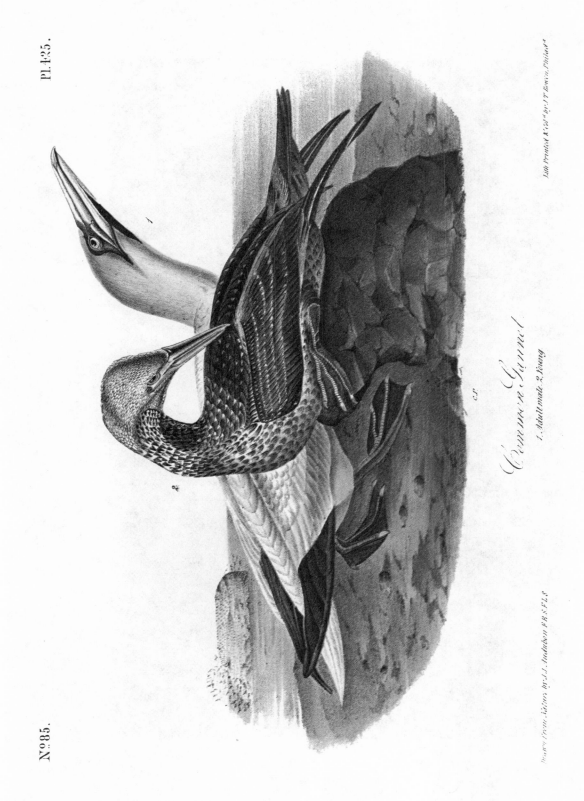

Common Gannet.
1. Adult male. 2. Young

Drawn from Nature by J.J. Audubon F.R.S. F.L.S.

Lith Printed & Col.d by J.T. Bowen, Phila.da

Pl. 427.

Tropic Bird
1. Male 2. Female

Drawn from Nature by J.J. Audubon, F.R.S. F.L.S

Lith Printed & Col'd by J T Bowen, Phila

Pl. 428.

Black Skimmer or Shearwater.
Male.

Drawn from Nature by J. J. Audubon, F.R.S. F.L.S.

Lith Printed & Cold by J.T. Bowen, Philad.ª

WEH

Arctic Tern.

Male

Drawn from Nature by J.J. Audubon, F.R.S. F.L.S.   Lith Printed & Colᵈ by J.T Bowen, Phila.

2.

1.

W.H.

Black Tern.
1. Adult. 2, Young.

Drawn from Nature by J.J. Audubon, F.R.S.F.L.S.   Lith. Printed & Colᵈ by J.T. Bowen, Philadᵃ

Pl. 429.

Cayenne Tern
Male.

Drawn from Nature by J.J.Audubon,F.R.S.F.L.S.

Lith. Printed & Col.ᵈ by J.T.Bowen, Philad.ᵃ

Common Tern

Male. Spring Plumage

Drawn from Nature by J.J. Audubon, F.R.S.F.L.S.   Lith. Printed & Col.º by J.T. Bowen, Phila.

Gull billed Tern Marsh Tern.

Male.

Drawn from Nature by J.J. Audubon, F.R.S.F.L.S.   Lith. Printed & Col.d by J.T. Bowen Philad.a

Pl. 434.

Havell's Tern

Adult.

Drawn from Nature by J. J. Audubon F.R.S. F.L.S

Lith Printed & Col.d by J.T.Bowen, Philad.a

453

Least Tern.

1. *Adult in Spring* 2. *Young.*

Drawn from Nature by J.J.Audubon, F.R.S.F.L.S.   Lithᵈ Printed & Colᵈ by J. T. Bowen, Philadᵃ

No. 88. Pl. 440.

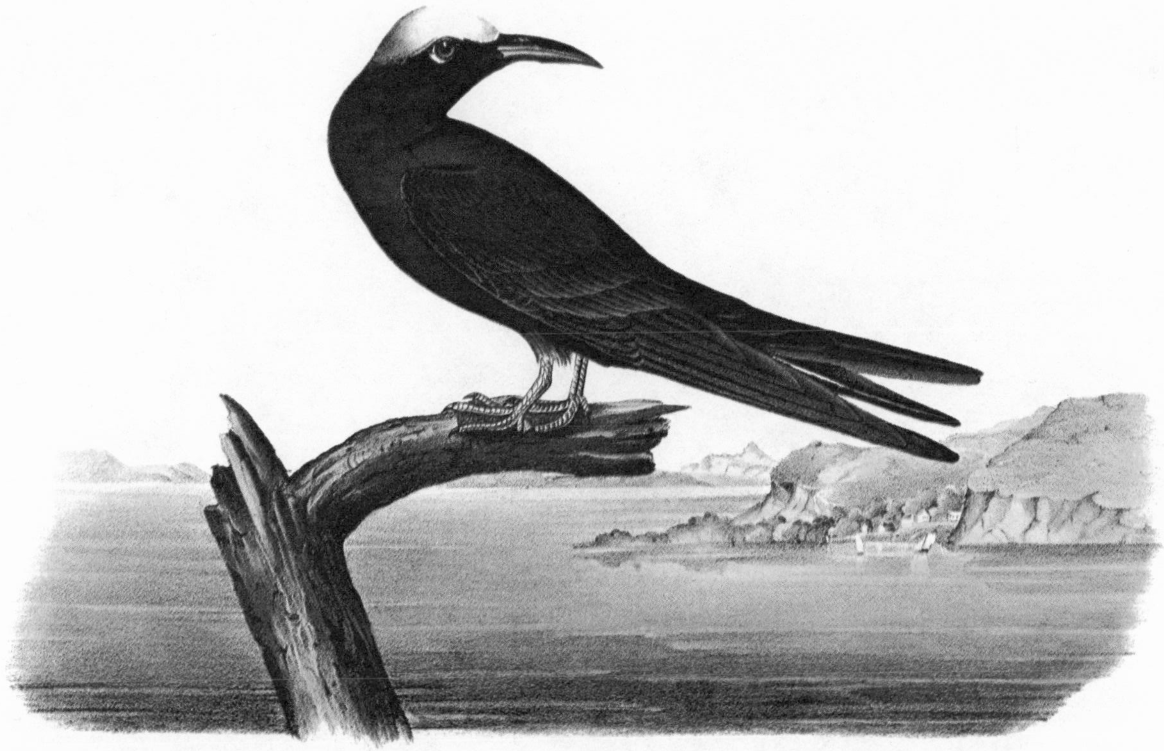

Noddy Tern

Male.

Drawn from Nature by J. J. Audubon, F.R.S. F.L.S.

Lith. Printed & Col.d by J. T. Bowen, Philad.a

Roseate Tern.

Male.

Drawn From Nature by J.J Audubon, F.R.S.F.L.S   Lith Printed & Col.d by J.T.Bowen, Philad.a

Pl. 431.

Drawn from Nature by J. J. Audubon, F.R.S. F.L.S.

Sandwich Tern.
Adult.

Lith. Printed & Col.d by J. T. Bowen, Phila.

Pl. 432.

N° 87.

Sooty Tern.

Drawn from Nature by J.J. Audubon. F.R.S. F.L.S

Lith. Printed & Col.d by J.T.Bowen, Phila

Pl. 435.

Trudeau's Tern.

Adult.

Drawn from Nature by J. J. Audubon F.R.S. F.L.S.

Lith. Printed & Col.d by J. T. Bowen, Phila.

Pl. 443.

Black-headed Gull.

1. Adult Male Spring Plumage. 2. Young First Autumn.

Drawn from Nature by J. J. Audubon, F.R.S. F.L.S.

Lith Printed & Col.d by J. T. Bowen. Phila.

Pl. 442.

Bonapartes Gull.

1. Male in Spring. 2. Female. 3. Young Bird. Autumn.

Drawn from Nature by J.J. Audubon. F.R.S.F.L.S

Lith. Printed & Col.d by J.T. Bowen Philad.a

Pl.446.

N°90.

Common American Gull. Ring-billed Gull.
1. Adult 2. Young

Drawn from Nature by J.J. Audubon, F.R.S. F.L.S

Fork-tailed Gull.
Male.

Drawn From Nature by J.J. Audubon, F.R.S.F.L.S

Lith. Printed & Col⁴ by J.T. Bowen, Philad⁴.

Pl.449.

W.E.H.

Glaucus Gull. Burgomaster.
1. Adult male. 2. Young first Autumn.

Drawn From Nature by J.J.Audubon, F.R.S.F.L.S

Lith.Printed & Col.ᵈ by J.T.Bowen, Phila.

W.E.H.

Great Black-backed Gull

Male

Drawn from Nature by J.J.Audubon, F.R.S.F.L.S.   Lith Printed & Col.d by J.T.Bowen, Philad.ª

W.E.H.

Herring or Silvery Gull

1. Adult in Spring. − 2. Young in Autumn.

Drawn from Nature by J.J.Audubon, F.R.S.F.L.S.   Lith. Printed & Col.ᵈ by J. T. Bowen, Philadelphia.

Pl. 445.

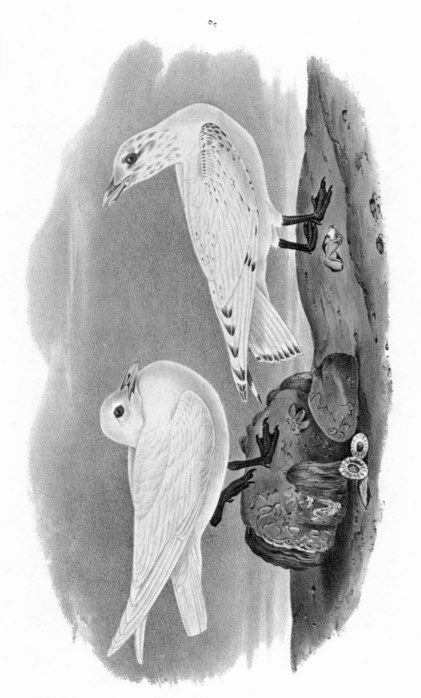

Ivory Gull.
1. Adult Male 2. Young second Autumn.

Drawn from Nature by J.J.Audubon, F.R.S F.L.S.

Lith Printed & Col.d by J. T. Bowen. Philad.a

No. 89.

Pl. 444.

Kittiwake Gull.
1. Adult. – 2. Young.

Drawn From Nature by J.J. Audubon, F.R.S. F.L.S.

Lith. Printed & Col.d by J.T. Bowen, Philad.a

Pl. 447.

No. 90.

2

1

White-winged Silvery Gull.
1. Male in Summer. 2. Young in Winter.

Drawn from Nature by J.J.Audubon, F.R.S.F.L.S.

Lith Printed & Col.rd by J.T.Bowen, Philadelphia

469

W.E.H.

Arctic Jager.

Drawn from Nature by J.J. Audubon, F.R.S. F.L.S.

Lith Printed & Col.d by J.T. Bowen, Philad.a

Pl. 451.

Pomarine Jäger.
Adult Female.

Drawn from Nature by J.J. Audubon, F.R.S.F.L.S.

Lith. Printed & Col.d by J.T. Bowen, Phila.

Pl. 452.

Richardson Jager.

1. Male Adult. 2. Young in Nov.

Drawn from Nature by J.J. Audubon, F.R.S. F.L.S.

Lith. Printed & Col.ᵈ by J.T. Bowen, Philad.ᵃ

Pl. 454.

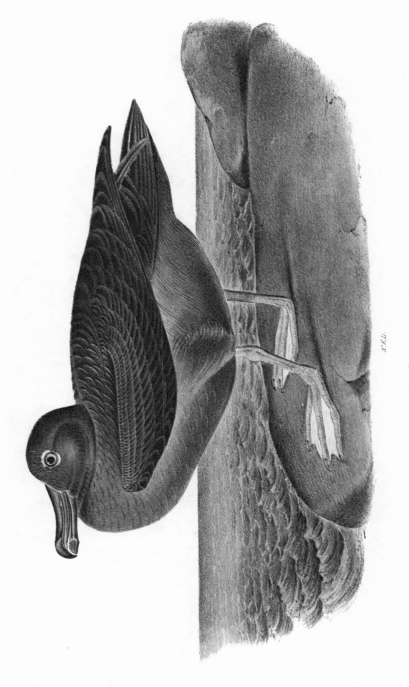

Drawn from Nature by J.J. Audubon. F.R.S. F.L.S.

N.E.

Dusky Albatross.

Lith. Printed & Col.d by J.T. Bowen, Philad.a

Pl. 455.

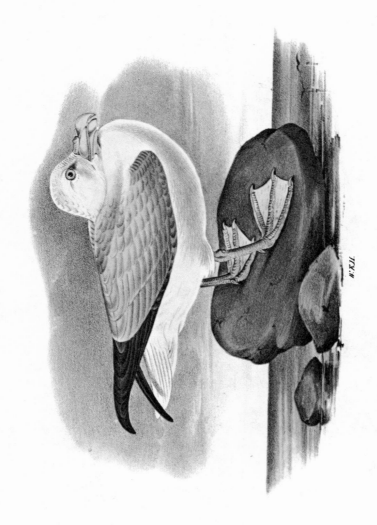

W.F.H.

Fulmar Petrel.

Adult Male Summer Plumage.

Drawn from Nature by J.J.Audubon, F.R.S.F.L.S.

Lith. Printed & Cold. by J.T.Bowen, Philad.a

474

Pl. 458.

W.E.H.

Dusky Shearwater.
Male in Spring

Drawn from Nature by J.J.Audubon, F.R.S.F.L.S.

Lith. Printed & Col.d by J.T.Bowen, Philad.a

N.º 92.

Pl. 457.

#W.H.

Manks Shearwater
Male

Drawn from Nature by J.J. Audubon, F.R.S.F.L.S

Lith Printed & Col.d by J.T. Bowen, Philad.ª

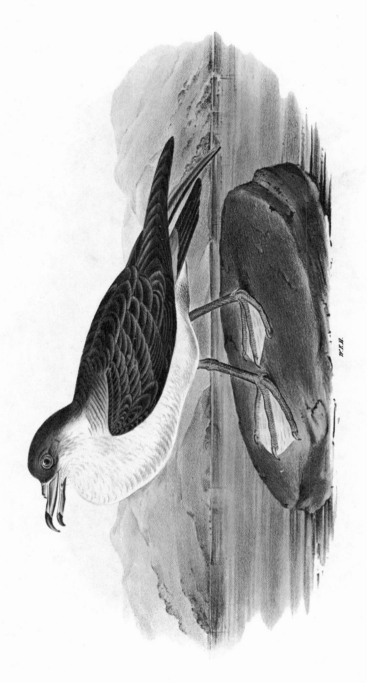

No. 92.

Pl. 456.

Drawn from Nature by J.J.Audubon, F.R.S.F.L.S.

Wandering Shearwater
Male

Lith Printed & Col.d by J.T.Bowen, Philad.a

477

Pl. 459.

1.

2.

Drawn from Nature by J. J. Audubon. F.R.S. F.L.S.

Leach's Petrel. 1. Forked-tailed Petrel.

1. Male. 2. Female.

Lith. Printed & Col.d by J.T.Bowen Philad.a

Pl. 461.

Least Petrel. Mother Carey's chicken?

1. Male. 2. Female.

Drawn from Nature by J. J. Audubon, F.R.S. F.L.S.

Lith. Printed & Cold. by J. T. Bowen, Philadelphia.

Pl.460.

2

1

WEH

Wilson's Petrel.__Mother Carey's chicken.
1. Male. 2. Female.

Drawn from Nature by J.J.Audubon, F.R.S. F.L.S.

Lith. Printed & Col.d by J.T. Bowen, Philad.a

Common or Arctic Puffin
1. Male. 2. Female

Drawn from Nature by J.J. Audubon, F.R.S.F.L.S

Lith. Printed & Col.d by J.T. Bowen, Philad.a

Pl. 463.

Large billed Puffin.
1. Male. 2. Female.

Drawn from Nature by J. J. Audubon, F.R.S.F.L.S.

Lith Printed & Cold by J. T. Bowen, Philada.

No. 93. Pl. 462.

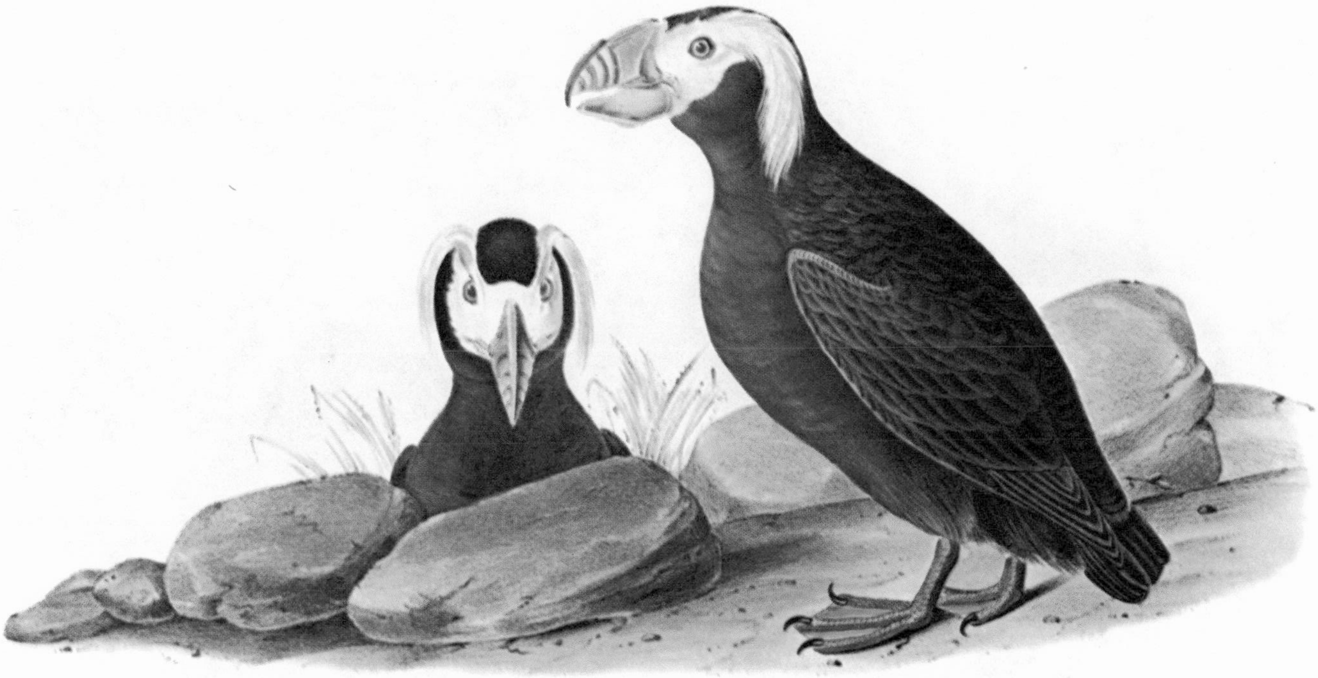

Tufted Puffin.

1. Male 2. Female.

Drawn from Nature by J. J. Audubon F.R.S. F.L.S.

Lith. Printed & Col.d by J. T. Bowen, Philad.a

Pl.465.

W.E.H.

Great Auk.

Adult.

Drawn from Nature by J.J.Audubon F.R.S.F.L.S

Pl. 466.

W.E.H.

Razor Billed Auk.

1. Male. 2. Female.

Drawn from Nature by J.J. Audubon, F.R.S.F.L.S

Lith Printed & Col.d by J.T Bowen Philad.a

Curled-crested Phaleris

Adult

Drawn from Nature by J. J. Audubon, P.R.S.F.L.S.

Lith Printed & Col.ª by J. T. Bowen, Philad.ª

Pl.468.

Knob-billed Phaleris.

Adult

Drawn from Nature by J. J. Audubon, F.R.S. F.L.S

Lith. Printed & Cold. by J. T. Bowen, Philad.ª

No. 94.

Pl. 469.

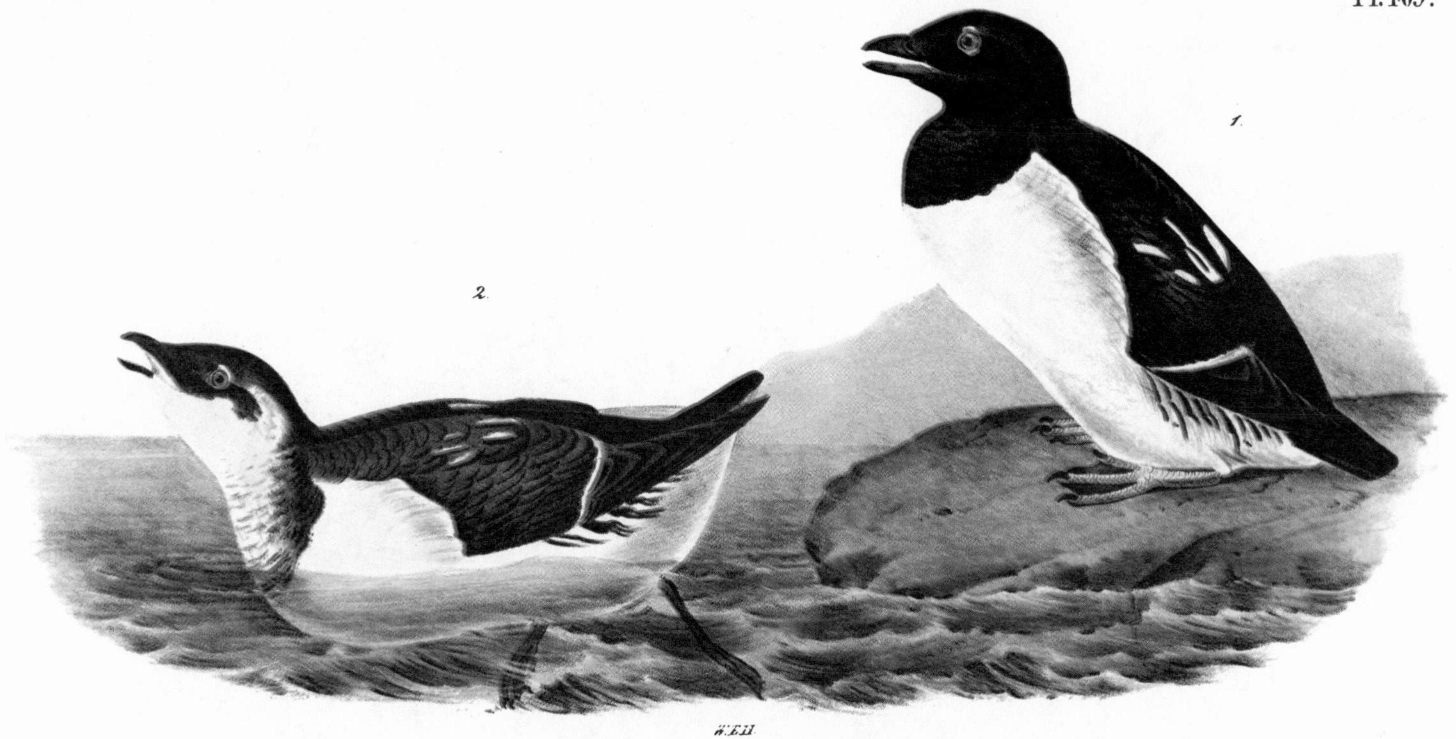

Little Auk – Sea dove.

1. Male. 2. Female

Drawn from Nature by J. J. Audubon, F.R.S. F.L.S.

Lith. Printed & Col.d by J. T. Bowen Phila.

No. 95.

Pl. 474.

Black Guillemot.

1. Male. — Summer Plumage. 2. Adult in Winter. 3. Young.

Drawn from Nature by J. J. Audubon, F.R.S.F.L.S.

Lith. Printed & Col.d by J. T. Bowen, Philad.a

489

Pl. 470.

N⁰ 94

Black throated Guillemot

Pl.473.

W.E.H.

Drawn from Nature by J.J.Audubon, F.R.S.F.L.S.

Foolish Guillemot.—Murre.

1. Male. 2. Female.

Lith Printed & Cold by J.T.Bowen, Philad.ª

Pl. 471.

Horned-billed Guillemot.
Adult.

Drawn from Nature by J.J. Audubon F.R.S.F.L.S

Lith.? Printed & Col.? by J.T. Bowen Philad.?

Pl. 472.

Large-billed Guillemot.
Male.

Drawn from Nature by J. J. Audubon, F.R.S. F.L.S

Lith. Printed & Col.d by J.T.Bowen, Philad.a

493

N?95.

Pl. 475.

W.R.H.

Slender-billed Guillemot.

1. Male. 2. Female

Drawn from Nature by J.J.Audubon, F.R.S.F.L.S.

Lith. Printed & Cold by J.T.Bowen, Philad.ᵃ

Pl. 477.

Drawn from Nature by J. J. Audubon, F. R. S. F. L. S.

Black-throated Diver.

1. Male. 2. Female. 3. Young in Ocber.

Lith. Printed & Col.d by J. T. Bowen, Phila.

PI. 476.

Great North Diver — Loon.

1. Adult ♂. 2. Young in Winter.

Drawn from Nature by J. J. Audubon F.R.S. F.L.S

Lith Printed & Col.d by J. T. Bowen Philad.a

Pl. 478.

W.E.B.

Red-throated Diver.

1. Male Summer Plumage. 2. do Winter 3. Female 4. Young

Drawn from Nature by J.J.Audubon, P.R.S.F.L.S

Lith. Printed & Col.^d by J. T. Bowen. Philad.^a

Pl. 479.

Crested Grebe.

1. Adult Male in Spring, 2. Young (first Winter.)

Drawn from Nature by J.J. Audubon, F.R.S. F.L.S.

Lith. Printed & Col.d by J.T. Bowen, Phila.

Pl. 482.

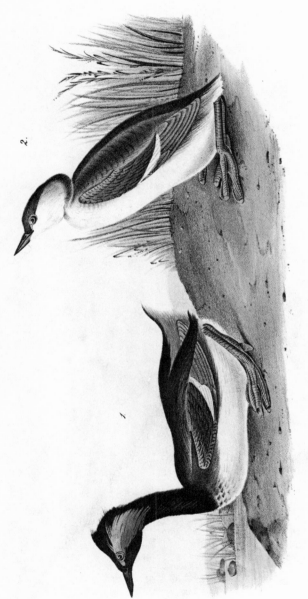

Eared Grebe.
1 Male 2 Young.—First Year

Drawn from Nature by J.J.Audubon, F.R.S.FL.S.

Lith. Printed & Col.ᵈ by J.T.Bowen, Philadᵃ

Pl. 481.

W.E.H.

Horned Grebe.

1. Adult Male. 2. Female in Winter.

Drawn from Nature by J.J.Audubon, F.R.S.F.L.S.

Lith. Printed & Col.ᵈ by J.T.Bowen, Philad.ᵃ

No. 97. Pl. 483.

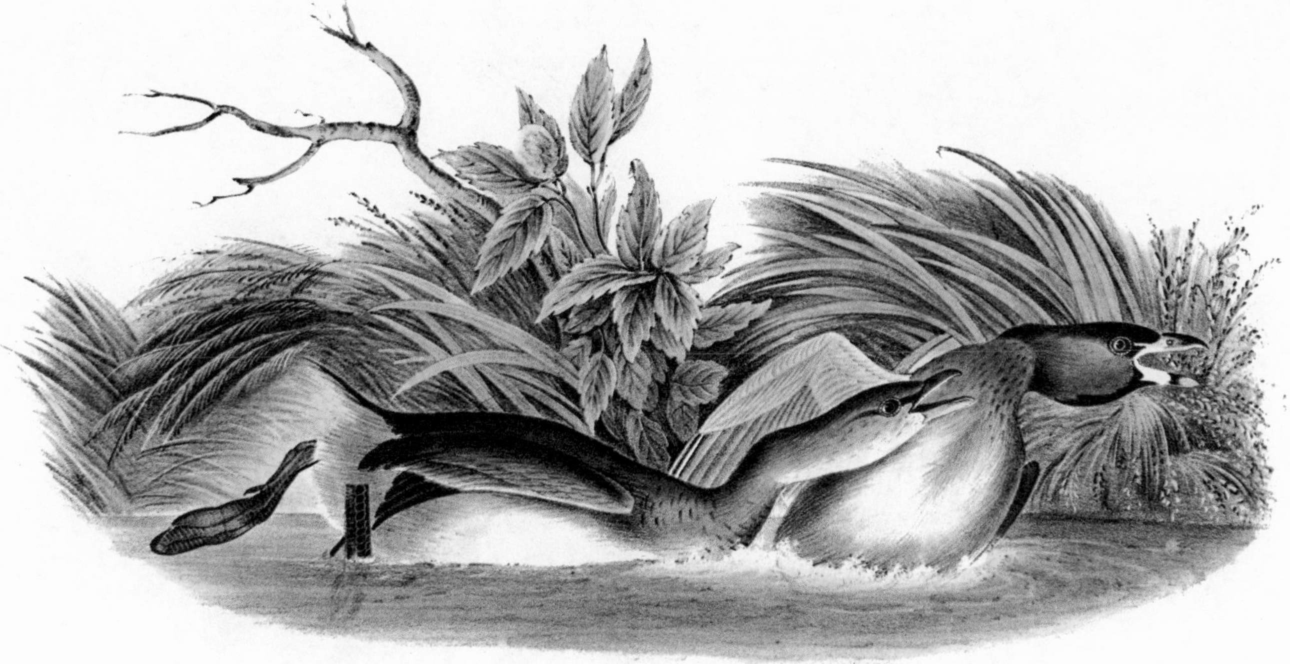

2 WEH 1

Pied-billed Dobchick.

Drawn from Nature by J. J. Audubon F.R.S.F.L.S.

1. Male, 2. Female.

Lith. Printed & Col.d by J. T. Bowen, Philad.a

Pl. 480.

Red-necked Grebe.

1. Adult Male Spring Plumage 2. Young Winter Plumage

Drawn from Nature by J.J. Audubon, F.R.S.V.L.S.

Lith Printed & Cold. by J.T. Bowen. Philada.

BOOK OF MAMMALS

Plate LXXVII

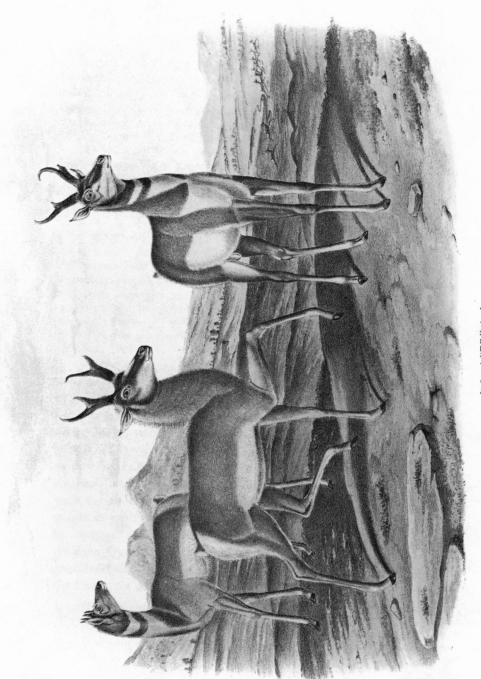

On Stone by Wm E. Hitchcock

Drawn from Nature by J.W. Audubon

Prong-Horned Antelope.

Lith. Printed & Cold by J.T. Bowen Phil.

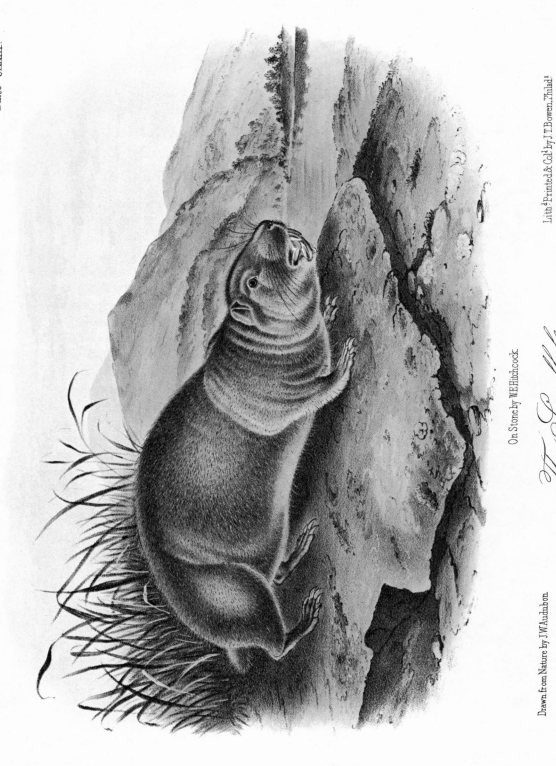

On Stone by W.E.Hitchcock.

Lith.ª Printed & Col.ª by J.T.Bowen, Philad.ª

The Sewellel.

Drawn from Nature by J.W.Audubon.

Plate CIII

Nº 21.

Drawn from Nature by J.W. Audubon.

Lith. Printed & Col.ª by J.T. Bowen, Phil.

Hoary Marmot. The Whistler.

Plate CVII

N°.22

508

Drawn from Nature by J.W. Audubon

Drawn on Stone by Wm E. Hitchcock

Lith. Printed & Col. by J.T.Bowen, Phil.

Lewis' Marmot.

Plate II

N°1.

Drawn on Stone by R. Trembly

Drawn from Nature by J. J. Audubon, F.R.S. F.L.S.

Maryland . Marmot . Woodchuck . Groundhog .

Old & Young .

Printed by Nagel & Weingärtner N.Y.

Plate (XXXIV.

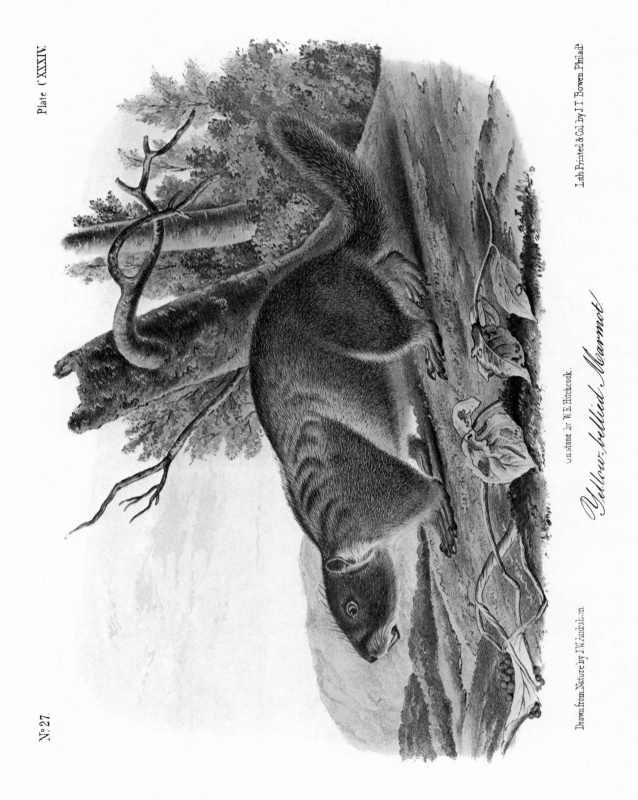

Drawn from Nature by J.W. Audubon.

On stone by W.E. Hitchcock.

Lith. Printed & Col. by J.T. Bowen Philad.ᵃ

Yellow-bellied Marmot.

Leconte's Pine Mouse.

Plate CXXIX

N.º 26

O. Store by M.º E. Hitchcock

Northern Meadow Mouse.

Drawn from Nature by J.W Audubon.

Lith. Printed & Col.ᵈ by J.T. Bowen, Phil

Plate CXLVII

Fig 1

Fig 2

Fig 3

On Stone by Wᵐ E. Hitchcock

Fig 1 *American Sousik* - Fig 2 *Oregon Meadow Mouse* - Fig 3 *Texan Meadow Mouse*

Drawn from Nature by J.W. Audubon

Lith. Printed & Col.ᵈ by J.T. Bowen, Phil

Plate CXXXV.

N°27.

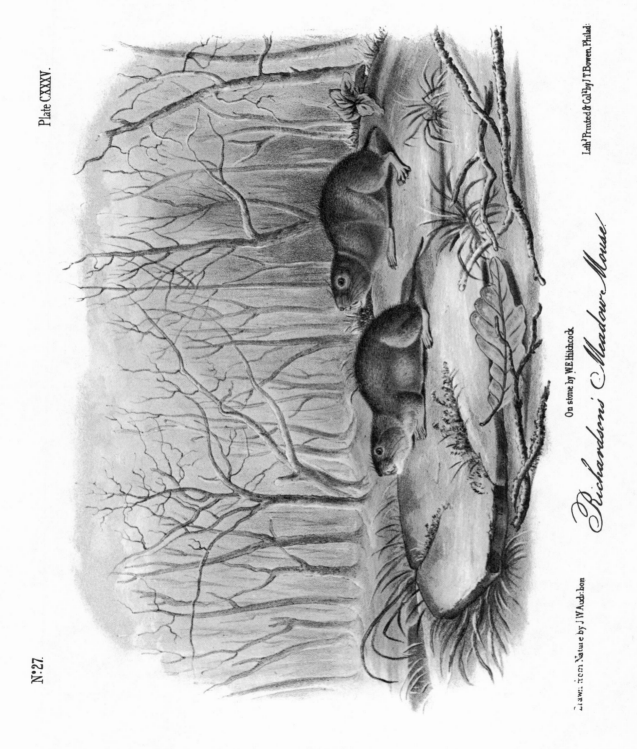

Draw: from Nature by J.W.Audubon

On stone by W.E.Hitchcock

Lith Printed & Col.by J.T.Bowen, Philad:

Richardson's Meadow Mouse.

514

Plate CXLIV

Fig. 1.

Fig 2.
On Stone by Wm E Hitchcock

Fig 3

Fig. 1. *Townsend's Arvicola.*   Fig. 2. *Sharp-nosed Arvicola.*   Fig. 3. *Bank Rat*

Drawn from Nature by J W Audubon

Lith. Printed & Colᵈ by J.T. Bowen, Phil

Plate XLV.

Drawn from Nature by J.J.Audubon, F.R.S. F.S.S.

Lith. Printed & Col.d by J.T. Bowen, Philada

Wilson's Meadow Mouse?

Plate CXV.

On Stone by W.E. Hitchcock

Lith Printed & Col.d by J.T.Bowen, Philad.a

Drawn from Nature by J. W. Audubon.

Yellow-cheeked Meadow Mouse.

517

On Stone by Wᵐ E. Hitchcock

Ring-Tailed Bassaris

Drawn from Nature by J W Audubon   Lith Printed & Colᵈ by J T Bowen, Phiᵗ

Plate LVI

On Stone by Wᵐ F. Hitchcock.

Drawn from Nature by J.J. Audubon, F.R.S. F.L.S.

American Bison or Buffalo

Lith. Printed & Col.d by J.T. Bowen, Phil.

519

Plate LVII

No 12

Drawn from Nature by J.J.Audubon, F.R.S.F.L.S.

On Stone by Wm E. Hitchcock

American Bison or Buffalo

Printed & Col.d by J.T. Bowen, Philad.a

520

Plate LXVII

N° 14

On Stone by W.E. Hitchcock

Drawn from Nature by J.W. Audubon

Black American Wolf

Lith Printed & Col'd by J.T. Bowen, Phil

Plate CXIII.

N.º 23

Drawn from Nature by J.W. Audubon

Drawn on Stone by Wᵐ. E. Hitchcock

Lith. Printed & Colᵈ. by J.T. Bowen, Phil

Esquimaux Dog.

Plate CXXXII

On stone by W.E.Hitchcock.

Hare-Indian Dog.

Drawn from Nature by J.W.Audubon

Lith Printed & Col⁴ by J.T Bowen, Philad⁴

Plate LXXI.

On Stone by Wᵐ. E. Hitchcock

Drawn from Nature by J.W. Audubon

Prairie Wolf.

Lith. Printed & Col.ᵈ by J.T. Bowen, Philad

Plate LXXXII.

On stone by W. E. Hitchcock.

Drawn from Nature by J. W. Audubon.

Red Texan Wolf.

Lith.ᵈ Printed & Col.ᵈ by J. T. Bowen, Philad.ᵃ

Plate LXXII

N°15

Drawn from Nature by J. W. Audubon

On Stone by W.ᵐ E. Hitchcock

White American Wolf

Lith Printed & Col.ᵈ by J.T. Bowen. P:..

526

Plate CXXVIII

Drawn from Nature by J.W. Audubon.

On Stone by Wᵐ. E. Hitchcock

Lith Printed & Colᵈ by J T Bowen: Phiᵃ

Rocky Mountain Goat.

Plate XLVI.

N° 10.

Drawn from Nature by J.J. Audubon, P.R.S.F.L.S

On Stone by R. Trembly

American Beaver.

Lith. Printed & Col.d by J.T.Bowen, Philada.

Plate LXXVII

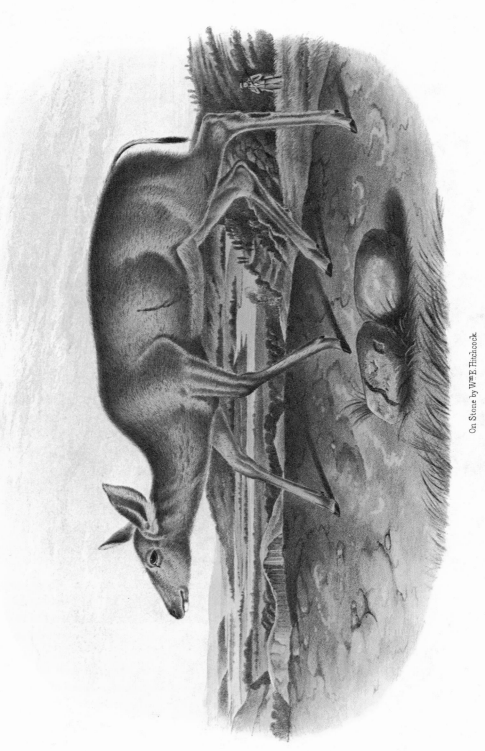

On Stone by Wᵐ E. Hitchcock

Drawn from Nature by J W Audubon

Black-tailed Deer

Lith. Printed & Colᵈ by J T Bowen, Phil

Plate CVI.

Drawn from Nature by J.W. Audubon.

On Stone by W.E. Hitchcock

Lith.Printed & Col.d by J.T. Bowen, Philad.a

Columbian Black Tailed Deer.

Plate LXXXI

Drawn from Nature by J.W. Audubon.

On Stone by Wm E. Hitchcock.

Lith. Printed & Cold by J.T. Bowen, Phil.

Common American Deer.

Plate CXXXVI

Drawn from Nature by J W Audubon

On Stone by Wᵐ E Hitchcock

Common or Virginian Deer.

Lith. Printed & Col⁴ by J T Bowen, Phil

Plate CXVIII.

N.º 24.

On Stone by W.E.Hitchcock.

Lithᵈ Printed & Colᵈ by J.T.Bowen,Philadᵃ.

Long-tailed Deer.

Drawn from Nature by J.W.Audubon.

Plate LXXVI

No. 16.

On Stone by W.E. Hitchcock

Moose Deer

Drawn from Nature by J.W.Audubon.

Lith.d Printed & Col.d by J.T.Bowen, Phila.d

Plate LXIX

N°14

On Stone by W.E. Hitchcock

Drawn from Nature by J.J Audubon F.R.S F.L.S

Common Star-Nose Mole.

Plate CXLVI

Drawn from Nature by J.W. Audubon

On Stone by Wᵐ. E. Hitchcock

Nine-banded Armadillo

Lith. Printed & Colᵈ by J.T. Bowen, Phil

On Stone by Wm E. Hitchcock

Virginian Opossum.

Drawn from Nature by J.J. Audubon, F.R.S.F.L.S   Lith Printed & Cold by Wm Bowen, Phil

Drawn from Nature by J.W Audubon

On Stone by Wm E. Hitchcock

Lith Printed & Co.^d by J.T Bowen, Phil

Pouched Jerboa Mouse

Plate XXXI

N°7

Drawn on Stone by R Trembly.

Collared Peccary.

Printed by Nagel & Weingærtner N.Y.

Drawn from Nature by J.J.Audubon F.R.S.FLS.

Plate LXII

Drawn from Nature by J.J.Audubon, F.R.S.F.L.S.

On Stone by W.E. Hitchcock

Lith. Printed & Col.d by J.T.Bowen, Phil.

American Elk.- Wapiti Deer.

Plate CXXXVII.

Drawn from Nature by J.W Audubon.

Sea Otter

Lith Printed & Col.ᵈ by J T Bowen, Philad.ª

N° 20.

Plate XCVII

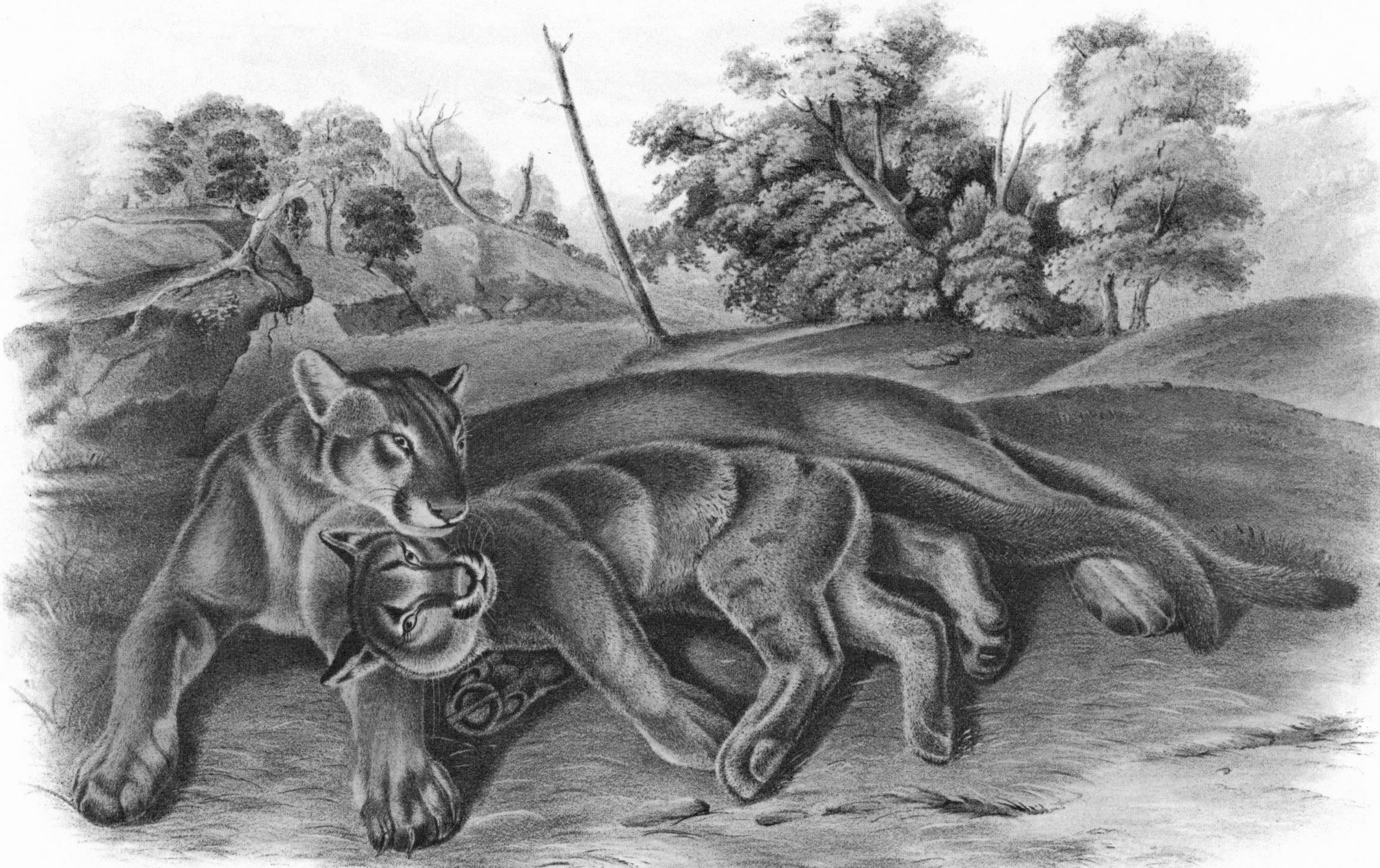

Drawn on Stone by Wm E. Hitchcock

Drawn from Nature by J. W. Audubon

The Cougar

Lith. Printed & Col^{d} by J. T. Bowen, Phil.

Female & Young.

Plate XCVI

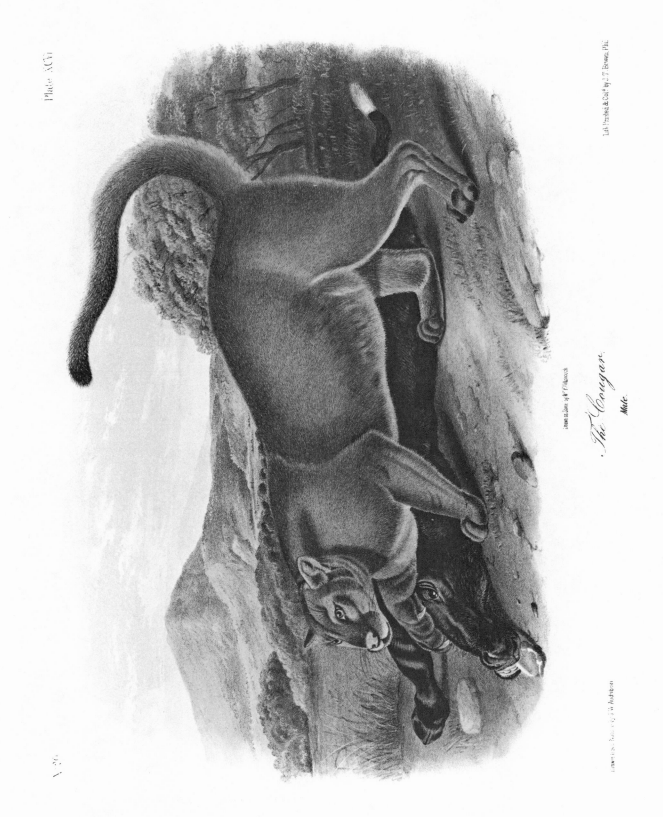

The Cougar.

Male.

Plate CI

Drawn from Nature by J. W. Audubon.

On Stone by W E. Hitchcock

The Jaguar.

Lith Printed & Col: by J. T Bowen, Philad.ª

N° 18 Plate LXXXVI

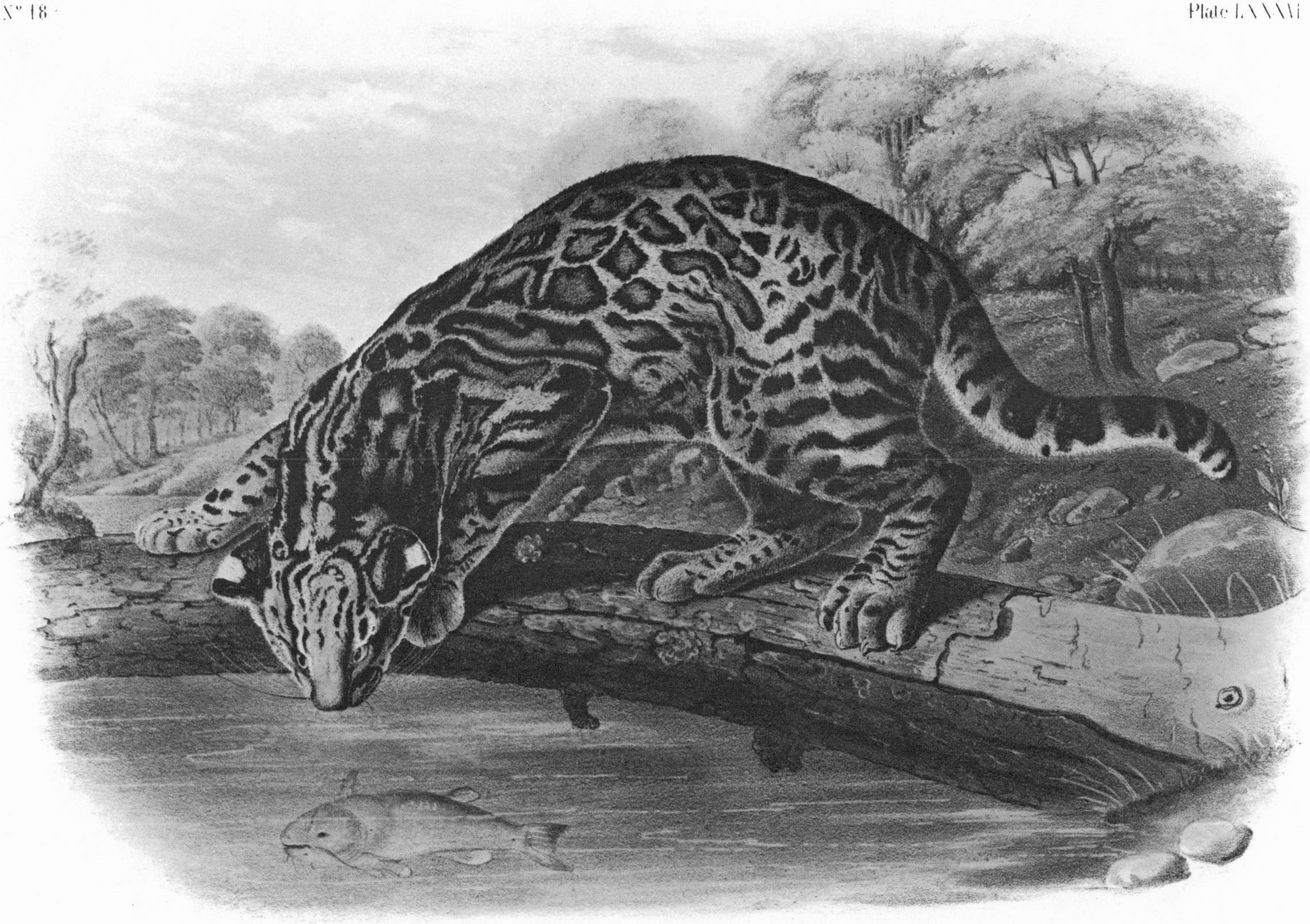

On Stone by Wm E. Hitchcock

Drawn from Nature by J. W. Audubon

Ocelot or Leopard-Cat.

Lith. Printed & Col.d by J. T. Bowen, Phila.

Plate XIII

Drawn from Nature by J.J.Audubon,F:R.S.F.LS

Drawn on Stone by Wᵐ E. Hitchcock

Lith. Printed & Colᵈ by J.T. Bowen, Phil

Mush. Rat.– Musquash.

Old & Young.

Plate CIX

Drawn on Stone by Wm E. Hitchcock

Drawn from Nature by J. W. Audubon

Lith Printed & Col^d by J T Bowen, Phil

Hudson's Bay Lemming

Plate CXX

Drawn from Nature by J.W.Audubon

Drawn on Stone by Wᵐ E Hitchcock

Lith. Printed & Colᵈ by J.T. Bowen, Phil

Fig: 1 Tawney Lemming.— Figs 2 & 3 Back's Lemming

Plate XXVI.

N.º 6.

Drawn on stone by R. Trembly

Wolverine.

Printed & Col.ᵈ by J.T Bowen, Philad.ᵃ

Drawn from Nature by J.J. Audubon, F.R.S.F.L.S.

Canada Porcupine.

Drawn from Nature by J.J.Audubon, F.R.S.F.L.S.   Lith.d, Printed & Col.d by J.T. Bowen, Philad.a

550

Plate LXXXIII

On Stone by Wm E. Hitchcock

Little Chief Hare.

Drawn from Nature by J.J.Audubon, F.R.S.F.L.S.

Lith. Printed & Cold by J.T. Bowen, Phil.

Plate CVIII

On Stone by W.B.Hitchcock

Bachman's Hare

Drawn from Nature by J.W.Audubon

Lith.ᵈ Printed & Col.ᵈ by J.T.Bowen,Philad.ᵃ

Plate LXIII

Drawn from Nature by J. J. Audubon, F.R.S. F.L.S.

On Stone by W. E. Hitchcock

Lith. Printed & Col.ᵈ by J.T. Bowen, Philad.ᵃ

Black-tailed Hare.

Plate CXII.

Drawn on stone by W.E. Hitchcock

Lith.ᵈ Printed & Col.ᵈ by J.T. Bowen, Philad.ᵃ

Californian Hare.

Drawn from Nature by J.W. Audubon.

Plate XXII

Drawn on Stone by R. Trembly.

Grey Rabbit.
Old & Young.

Drawn from Nature by J.J.Audubon, F.R.S, F.L.S.

Printed by Nagel & Weingærtner, N.Y.

Plate XVIII

Drawn on Stone by R Trembly

Marsh Hare.

Drawn from Nature by J.J.Audubon. F.R.S.F.L.S.

Printed by Nagel & Weingærtner N.Y.

Plate XI

Northern Hare. (Old & Young)

Summer pelage.

Drawn from Nature by J.J.Audubon F.R.S.F.L.S.

Drawn on Stone by R.Trembly.

Printed by Nagel & Weingærtner N.Y

Nº3.

Plate XII

N°3.

Northern Hare

Winter pelage.

Drawn from Nature by J.J.Audubon F.R.S.F.L.S.
Drawn on Stone by R.Trembly.

Printed by Nagel & Weingærtner, N.Y.
Colored by J.Lawrence

558

Plate XCIV

On Stone by Wᵐᴱ Hitchcock

Lith. Printed &Colᵈ by J.T.Bowen, Phil

Drawn from Nature by J.W. Audubon

Nuttall's Hare.

Plate XXXII.

Drawn from Nature by J.J.Audubon, F.R.S.F.L.S.

Drawn on stone by R. Trembly

Polar Hare

Printed & Col.ᵈ by J.T.Bowen, Philadᵃ.

Plate XXXVII.

N.º 8.

Drawn on Stone by R. Trembly

Drawn from Nature by J. J. Audubon, F.R.S. F.L.S.

Lith Printed & Col.ᵈ by J. T. Bowen, Phil.

Swamp Hare

Male.

Plate CXXXIII.

Drawn from Nature by J. W. Audubon.

On stone by W.E. Hitchcock.

Texian Hare.

Lith Printed & Col.ᵈ by J.T. Bowen. Philadᵃ

Plate III.

No I.

Drawn from Nature by J.J.Audubon F.R.S.F.L.S.

Drawn on Stone by R.Trembly

Townsend's Rocky Mountain Hare.
Male & Female.

Printed by Nagel & Weingærtner N.Y.

563

Plate LXXXVIII.

N.° 18.

On Stone by W E Hitchcock

Drawn from Nature by J.J Audubon, F R S. FLS.

Lith.ᵈ Printed & Col.ᵈ by J.T. Bowen, Philad.ᵃ

Worm-wood Hare.

Plate LI

Drawn from Nature by J. J. Audubon, F.R.S. F.L.S.

Canada Otter.

Lith. Printed & Col.d by J. T. Bowen, Philad.a

Plate CXXII

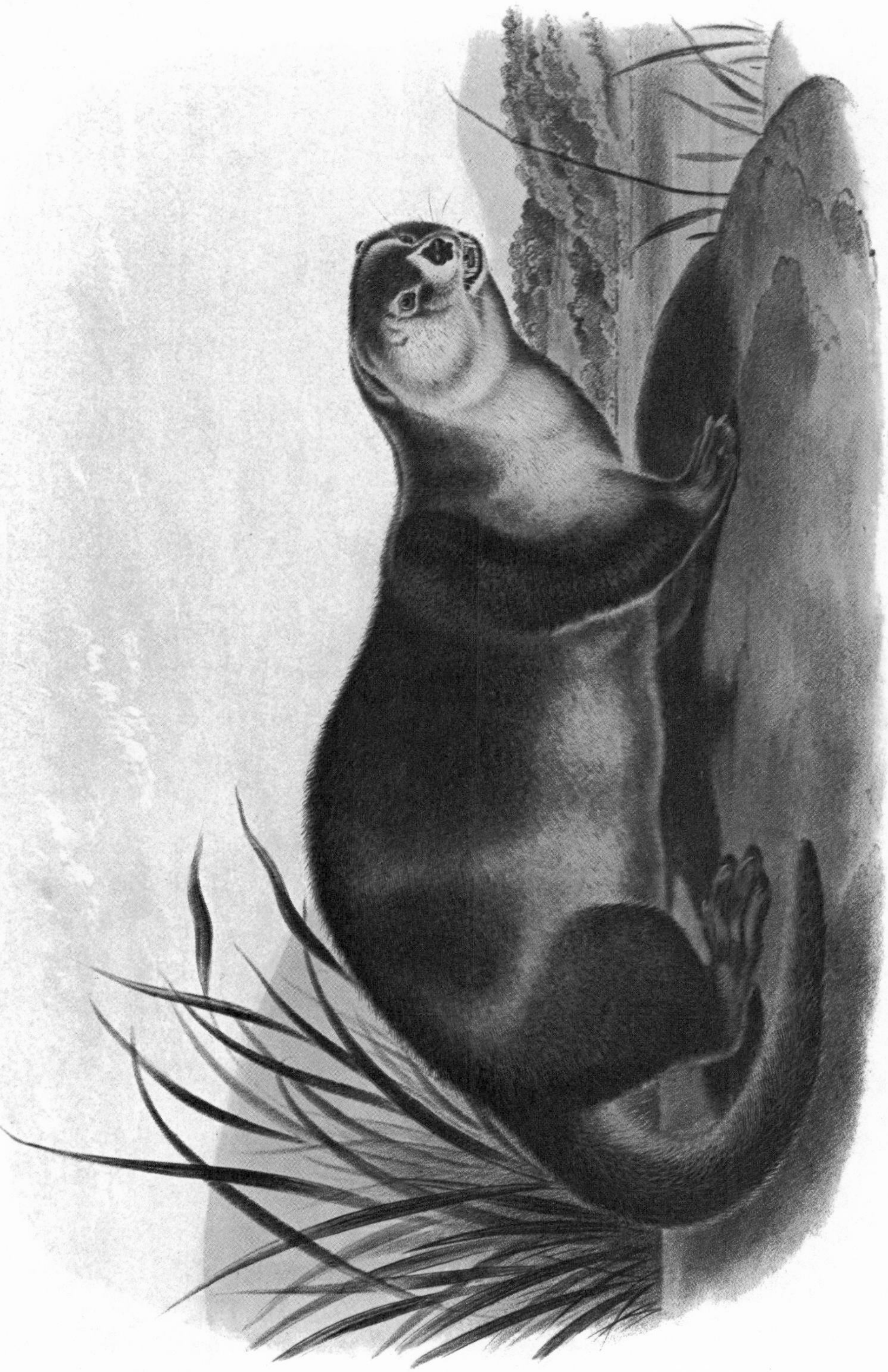

On Stone by Wm E Hitchcock

Canada Otter

No. 25

Drawn from Nature by J.W.Audubon

Plate XVI

N°.4

Drawn on Stone by R Trembly

Printed by Nagel & Weingærtner N.Y.

Canada Lynx.
Male

Drawn from Nature by J.J Audubon. F.R.S.F.L.S.

Plate I.

№ 1.

Drawn from Nature by J.J.Audubon.F.R.S.F.L.S.

Drawn on Stone by R Trembly

Common American Wild-cat.
Male.

Printed by Nagel & Weingærtner N.Y.

568

Plate XCII

Nº19

Drawn from Nature by J W Audubon.

On Stone by Wᵐ E. Hitchcock

Texian Lynx.

Lith. Printed & Colᵈ by J.T.Bowen, Phil

Plate XLVII

Drawn from Nature by J.J.Audubon, F.R.S.F.L.S

American Badger

Lith. Printed & Col.ᵈ by J.T. Bowen, Philadᵃ

Common American Skunk.

Drawn from Nature by J.J. Audubon, F.R.S. F.L.S.   Lith Printed & Col⁴ by J.T. Bowen, Philad⁴

On Stone by W.E.Hitchcock.

Large-Tailed Skunk.

Drawn from Nature by J.W.Audubon.

Lith Printed & Col⁴ by J.T.Bowen, Philad⁴

572

No. 11

Plate LIII

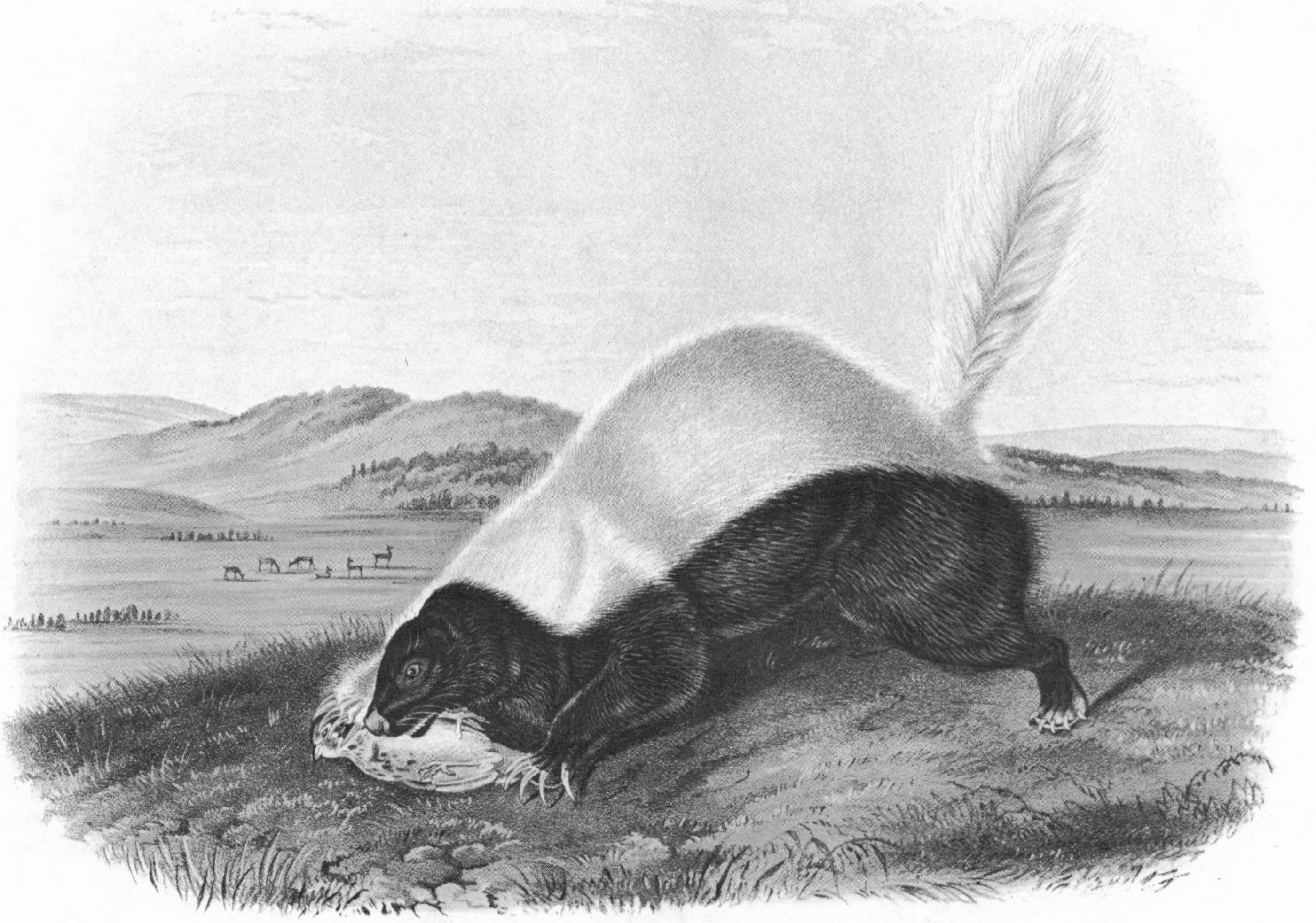

Drawn from Nature by J.J. Audubon, F.R.S.F.L.S.

On Stone by Wm E. Hitchcock

Lith. Printed & Cold. by J.T. Bowen, Phil.

Texan Skunk.

Plate LXXV

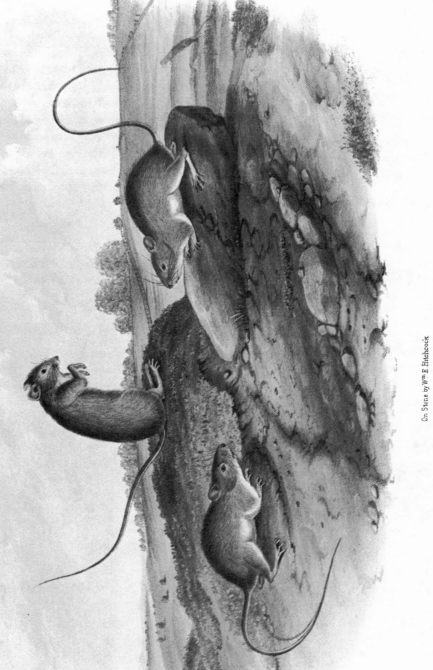

Drawn from Nature by J. J. Audubon FRS. FLS.

On Stone by Wm E. Hitchcock

Jumping Mouse.

Lith Printed & Col^d by J. T. Bowen, Ph.

574

Plate XL

Drawn from Nature by J.J. Audubon. F.R.S. F.L.S.

Drawn on Stone by Wm E. Hitchcock

Lith Printed & Cold by J.T. Bowen, Philada

White Footed Mouse.

Drawn on Stone by R Trembly.

Black Rat

Old & Young.

Drawn from Nature by J.J.Audubon.F.R.S.F.L.S.

Printed by Nagel & Weingærtner, N.Y.

Plate LIV

Drawn from Nature by J.J. Audubon, F.R.S.F.L.S.

On Stone by Wm E. Hitchcock

Lith. Printed & Col^d by J.T. Bowen, Phil.

Brown or Norway Rat

N° 18

Plate XC

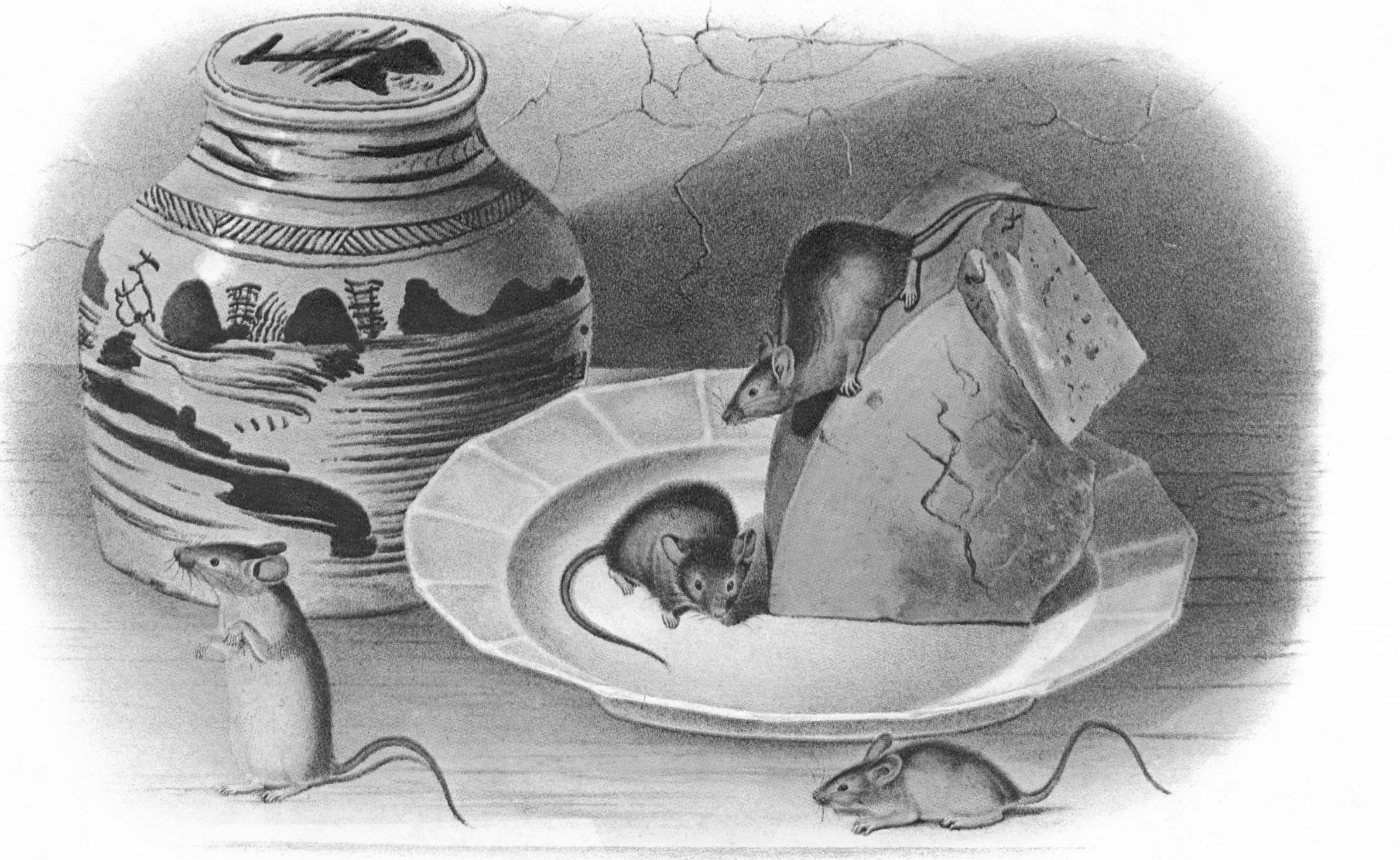

On Stone by W^{m} E Hitchcock

Drawn from Nature by J.W Audubon.

Common Mouse.

Lith Printed & Col^{d} by J.T. Bowen, Phil

Plate LXV.

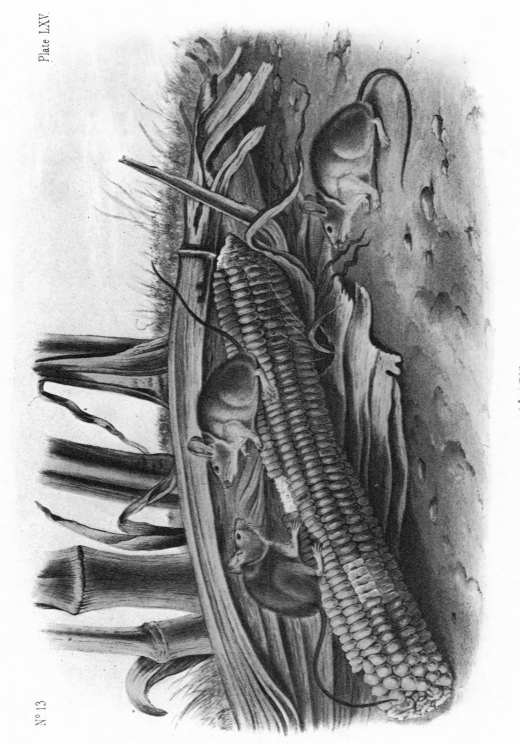

Drawn from Nature by J. J. Audubon F.R.S.F.L.S.

On Stone by W. E. Hitchcock

Little Harvest Mouse.

Plate C.

Drawn from Nature by J.W. Audubon.

On Stone by W.E. Hitchcock.

Lith Printed & Cold by J.T. Bowen, Philad.ª

Missouri Mouse.

Plate XCV

On Stone by Wᵐ E Hitchcock

Drawn from Nature by J.W. Audubon.

Lith. Printed & Colᵈ by J.T Bowen; Phil

Orange Colored Mouse

Drawn on Stone by W. E. Hitchcock

Pennant's Marten or Fisher.

Drawn from Nature by J.J Audubon, F.R.S.F.L.S   Lith.ᵈ Printed & Col.ᵈ by J. T. Bowen, Philad.ᵃ

Drawn from Nature by J W Audubon

On Stone by W E Hitchcock

Pine Marten

Lith. Printed & Col. by J. T. Bowen, Phil.

583

Plate IV

Drawn on Stone by Wᵐ. E. Hitchcock

Florida Rat.

Male, Female & Young of different ages

Drawn from Nature by J.J.Audubon, F.R.S.FL S

Lith Printed & Colᵈ by J T.Bowen, Phil

Plate XXIX

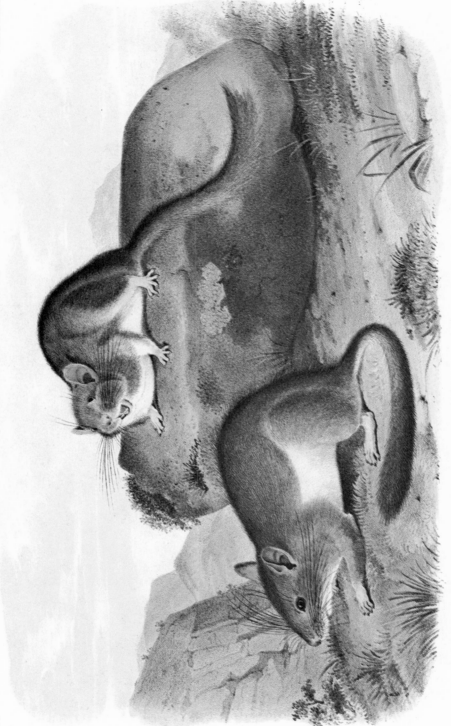

Drawn from Nature by J.J.Audubon. FRS.F.L.S.

Drawn on Stone by R.Trembly

Rocky Mountain Neotoma

Printed by Nagel &Weingærtner N.Y.

N.º 23

Plate CXI.

Drawn from Nature by J.W. Audubon.

Drawn on Stone by Wᵐ E. Hitchcock

Musk Ox.

Lith. Printed & Colᵈ by J.T. Bowen, Phil.

Plate LXXIII

Drawn from Nature by J. W. Audubon

On Stone by Wᵐ E. Hitchcock

Lith. Printed & Colᵈ by J.T Bowen, Phil.

Rocky Mountain Sheep.

Plate CLV.

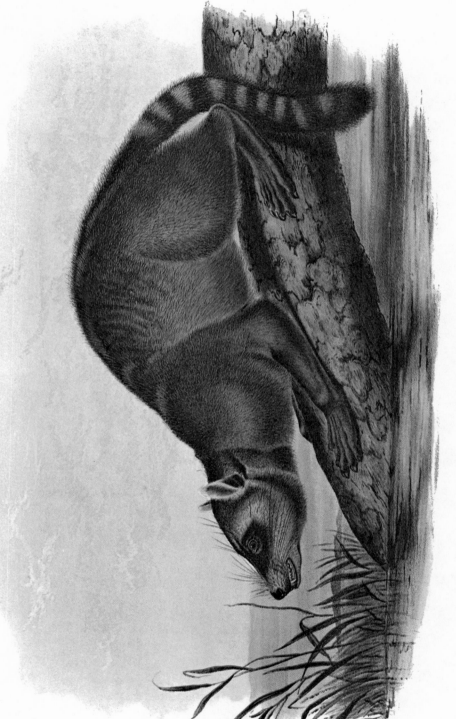

On Stone by Wᵐ E. Hitchcock.

Crab-eating Racoon.

Drawn from Nature by J.W. Audubon

Lith. Printed & Colᵈ by J.T. Bowen, Phil

On Stone by W. H. Hitchcock

Raccoon.

Drawn from Nature by J. W. Audubon   Lith. Printed & Col.ᵈ by J. T. Bowen, Phil

N° 29

Plate CXLII.

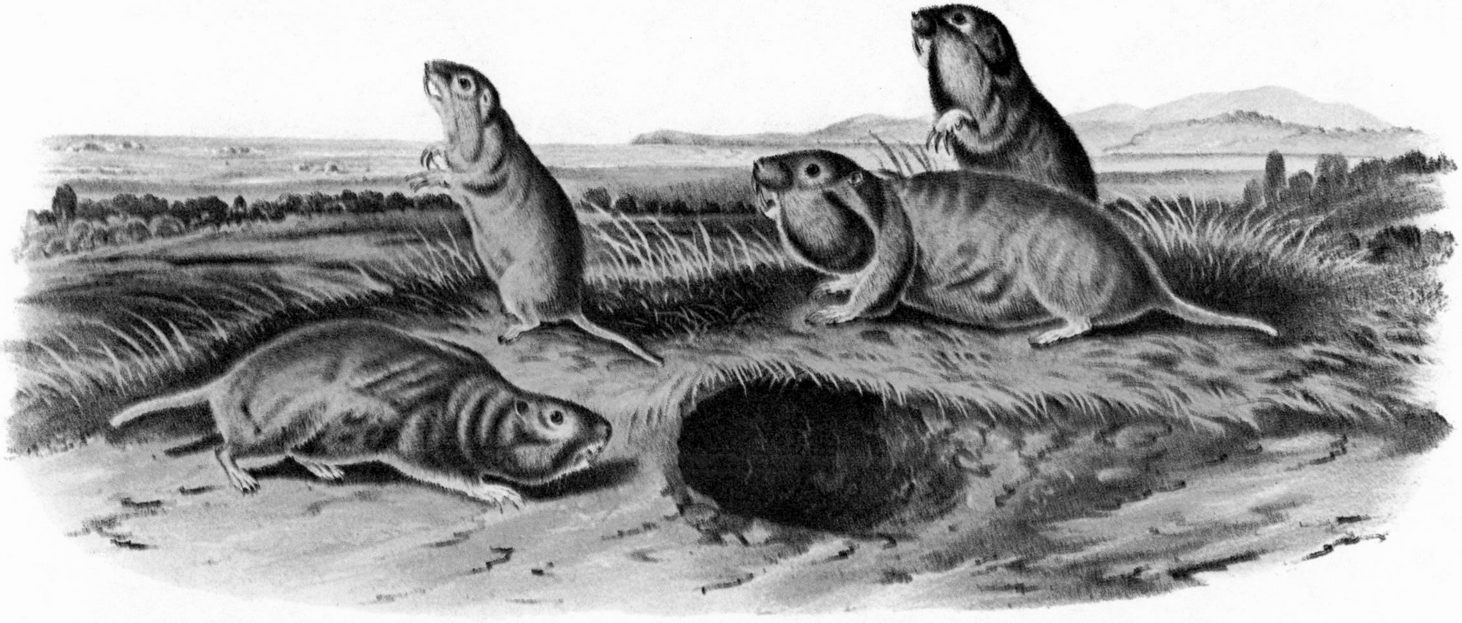

Drawn from Nature by J W Audubon

On Stone by Wm E. Hitchcock

Lith. Printed & Col^d by J. T. Bowen, Phil^a

The Camas Rat

No 9.

Plate XLIV

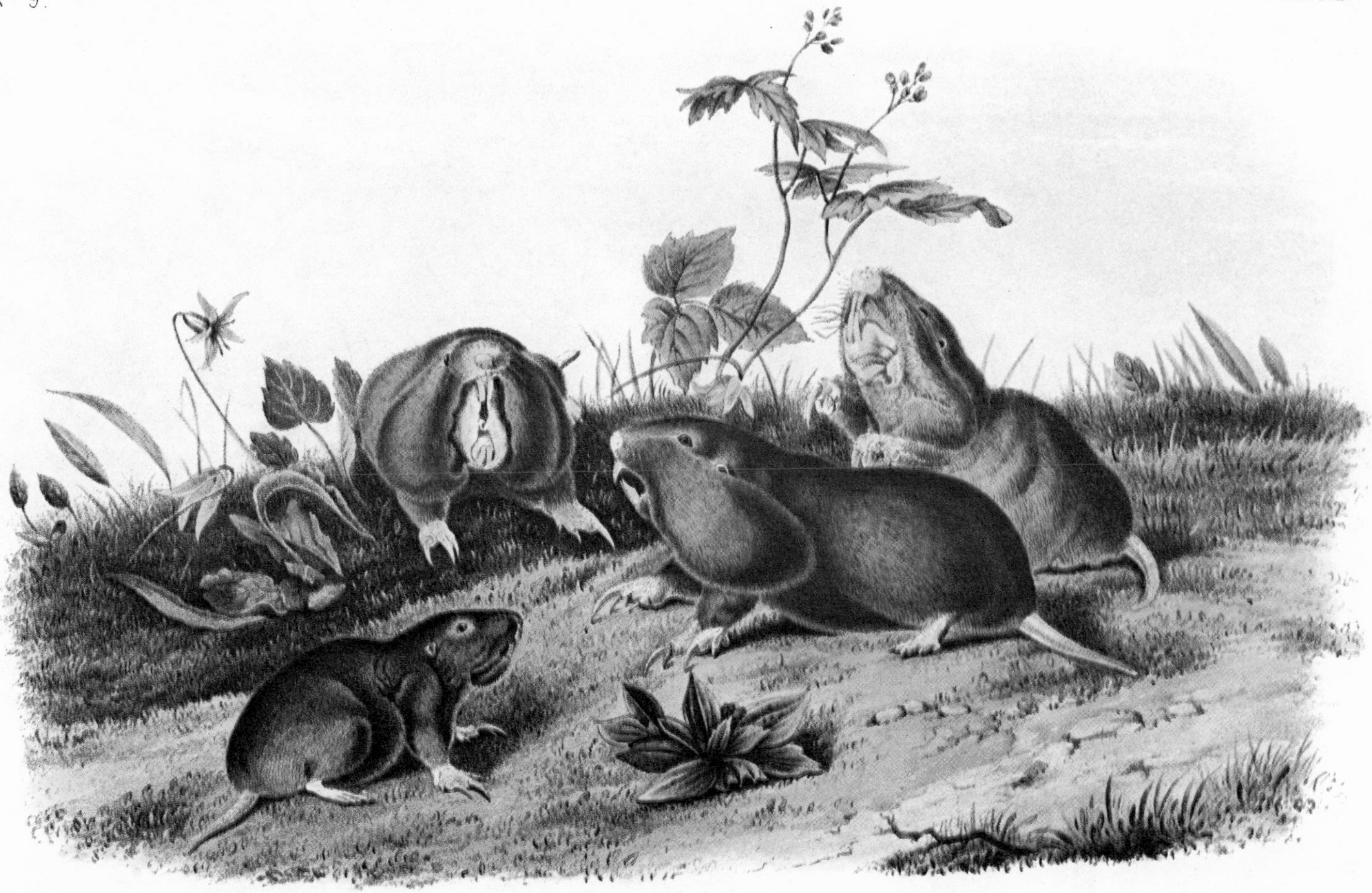

Canada Pouched Rat.

Drawn from Nature by J. J. Audubon F.R.S. F.L.S.

Lith. Printed & Col^{d} by J. T. Bowen, Philad^{a}.

N° 21

Plate CV.

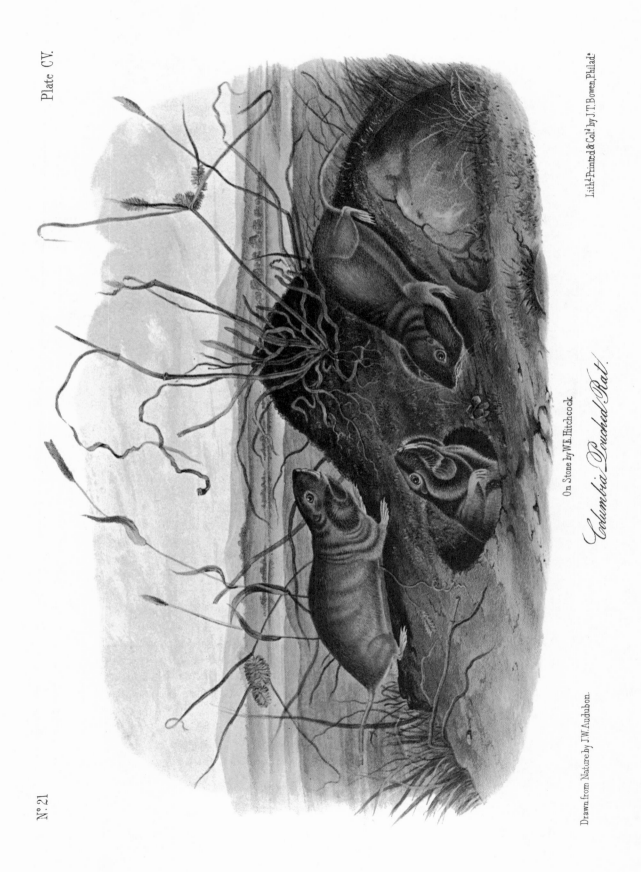

Drawn from Nature by J.W. Audubon.

On Stone by W.E. Hitchcock

Lith⁴.Printed & Col⁴ by J.T.Bowen,Philad⁴.

Columbia Pouched Rat.

On Stone by W.E.Hitchcock.

Drawn from Nature by J.W.Audubon.

Mole-shaped Pouched Rat.

Lith: Printed & Col.ᵈ by J.T.Bowen Philadᵃ.

Plate CL.

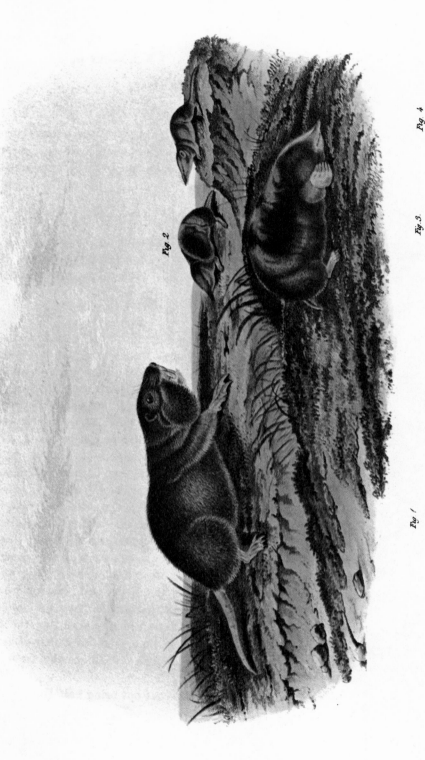

Fig. 1

Fig. 2

Fig. 3.

Fig. 4

On Stone by Wm E Hitchcock

Fig 1 Southern Pouched Rat. Fig 2. Dekay's Shrew. Fig 3. Long-Nosed Shrew. Fig 4 Silvery Shrew Mole.

Drawn from Nature by J. W. Audubon

Lith. Printed & Col.d by J.T. Bowen, Phil

Drawn on Stone by R. Trembly

Common Flying Squirrel
1,2 Males, 3,4 Females, 5 Young

Drawn from Nature by J.J.Audubon F.R.S. F.L.S.   Printed by Nagel & Weingærtner N Y

Drawn on Stone by Wᵐ E. Hitchcock

Oregon Flying Squirrel.

Drawn from Nature by J.J.Audubon,F.R.S.F.L.S.

Lithᵈ Printed & Colᵈ by J.T.Bowen,Phil.

Fig 1. Severn River Flying Squirrel

Fig 2. Rocky Mountain Flying Squirrel

Plate XCIII

On Stone by Wm E. Hitchcock

Lith. Printed & Col'd by J.T. Bowen. Phil.

Drawn from Nature by J.W. Audubon.

Black Footed Ferrett

Plate LX

N°. 12

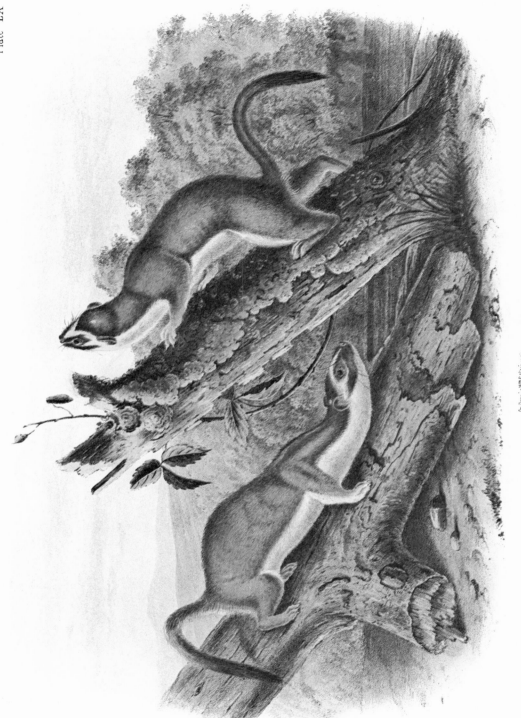

On Stone by Wm E Hitchcock

Lith Printed & Col. by J T Bowen Philad.

Bridled Weasel.

Drawn from Nature by J.J.Audubon. F.R.S.F.L.S.

Plate LXIV

Drawn from Nature by J. W. Audubon.

On Stone by W. H. Hitchcock

Lith Printed & Col.ᵈ by J. T. Bowen, Phil.ᵃ

Little American Brown Weasel.

Plate CXL.

N°.28.

On stone by W.E.Hitchcock

Drawn from Nature by J.W.Audubon.

Lith⁴ Printed & Col⁴ by J.T. Bowen Philad⁴

Little Nimble Weasel.

Plate XXXIII.

Drawn from Nature by J.J.Audubon, F.R.S. F.L.S.

Drawn on stone by R. Trembly

Mink.

Male & Female

Printed & Colᵈ by J.T.Bowen, Philadᵃ

Plate CXXIV

Drawn from Nature by J W Audubon

On Stone by Wm E. Hitchcock

Lith. Printed & Col^d by J T Bowen, Phil.

Mountain Brook Mink.

No. 30

Plate CXLVIII

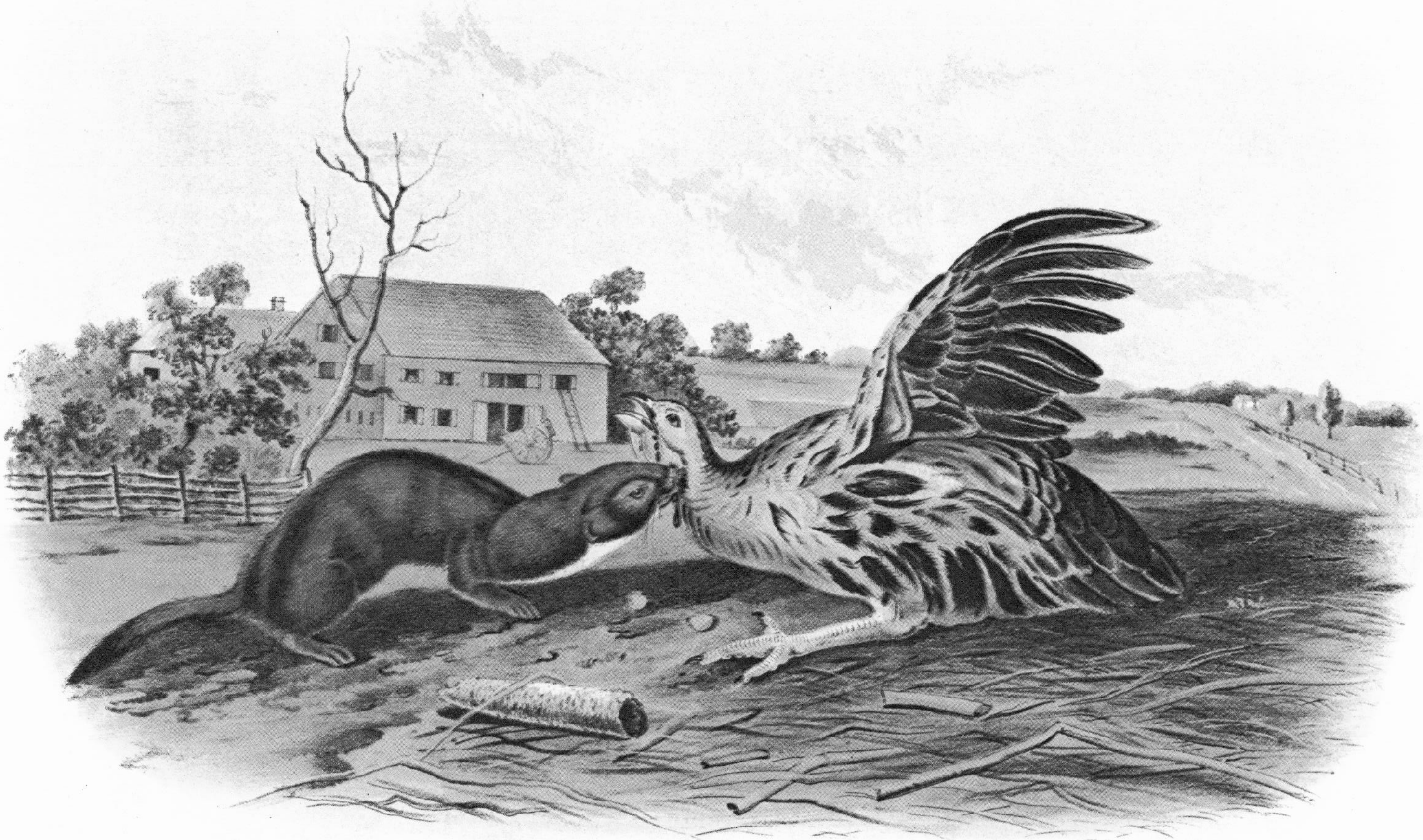

On Stone by Wm E. Hitchcock

Drawn from Nature by J.W. Audubon

Tawny Weasel.

Lith. Printed & Cold. by J.T. Bowen, Phil.

Plate LIX.

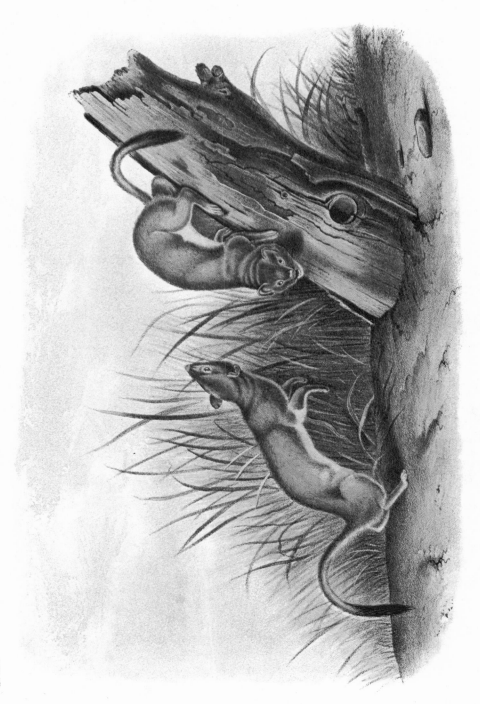

Drawn from Nature by J.J. Audubon FRSFLS

White Weasel; Stoat.

Lith.ᵈ Printed & Col.ᵈ by J.T. Bowen. Philad.ᵃ

Plate CXXVI

On Stone by Wᵐ E. Hitchcock

Lith. Printed & Colᵈ by J.T.Bowen, Phil.

Caribou or American Rein Deer.

Drawn from Nature by J.W. Audubon.

Plate LXXIV

Drawn from Nature by J. J. Audubon, FRS FLS

On Stone by W. E. Hitchcock

Lith. Printed & Col'd by J. T. Bowen, Phil'a

Brewer's Shrew Mole

Plate X

Drawn on Stone by W E Hitchcock.

Lith.d Printed & Col.d by J.T.Bowen, Philad.a

Drawn from Nature by J.J.Audubon F.R.S F.L.S

Common American Shrew Mole.
Male & Female

Plate CXLV

On Stone by Wᵐ E. Hitchcock

Lith. Printed & Col.ᵈ by J.T. Bowen, Phil.

Townsend's Shrew Mole

Drawn from Nature by J.W. Audubon

Black Squirrel.

Drawn from Nature by J.J.Audubon, F.R.S F.L.S.   Lith⁴,Printed & Col⁴ by J.T. Bowen, Philad.ᵃ.

Drawn on Stone by R. Trembly.

Carolina Grey Squirrel.
Male & Female.

Drawn from Nature by J.J. Audubon F.R.S.F.L.S.

Printed by Nagel & Weingærtner, N.Y.

Cat Squirrel

Drawn from Nature by J.J.Audubon FRS FLS   Printed by Nagel & Weingærtner NY

Drawn on Stone by R.Trembly   Colored by J Lawrence

Plate CLIII

N°. 31

Fig. 1

Fig. 2

Fig. 1. Abert's Squirrel. — Fig. 2. California Grey Squirrel.

Drawn from Nature by J.W. Audubon.

Lith Printed & Col.d by J.T. Bowen, Phil.

On Stone by Wᵐ E. Hitchcock.

Collies Squirrel

Drawn from Nature by J.W. Audubon   Lith. Printed & Colᵈ by J.T. Bowen, Pᵗ.

Drawn on Stone by J. Trembly

Downy Squirrel.

Drawn from Nature by J.J.Audubon F.R.S F.L.S.

Printed by Nagel & Weingærtner N.Y.

On Stone by Wᵐ. H. Hitchcock

Douglass Squirrel.

Drawn from Nature by J.J.Audubon. F.R.S.F.L.S.   Lith. Printed & Colᵈ by J.T.Bowen, Philᵃ.

On Stone by W.E.Hitchcock.

Dusky Squirrel.

Drawn from Nature by J.W.Audubon.   Lith.ª Printed & Col.ª by J.T.Bowen, Philad.ª

Fig. 1 Fremont's Squirrel. — Fig. 2 Sooty Squirrel.

On Stone, H. C. La Costa

Fox Squirrel.

Drawn from Nature by J.J Audubon, F.R.S.F.L.S. Lith Printed & Colᵈ by J.T. Bowen, Phil

Drawn on Stone by W.E. Hitchcock.

Hare Squirrel.

Hudson's Bay Squirrel - Chickaree - Red Squirrel.

Drawn from Nature by J.J.Audubon F.R.S.,F.L.S.   Printed by Nagel & Weingærtner N.Y.

Drawn on Stone by R Trembly.   Colored by J.Lawrence

Drawn on stone by R.Trembly

Long Haired Squirrel.

Drawn from Nature by J.J.Audubon, F.R.S. F.L.S.   Printed & Colᵈ by J.T. Bowen, Philad

Stone by Wᵐ E. Hitchcock

Migratory Squirrel

Drawn from Nature by J.J.Audubon,F.R.S.F.L.S.   Lith.Printed & Colᵈ by J.T.Bowen,Phil

On Stone by W.E. Hitchcock

Orange-bellied Squirrel.

Drawn from Nature by J.J.Audubon, P.P.S.I.I.S.   Lithᵈ Printed & Colᵈ by J. T. Bowen, Philadᵃ

Red-Bellied Squirrel.

Drawn from Nature by J.J.Audubon, F.R.S.FL.S.   Lith.ᵈ Printed & Col.ᵈ by J.T.Bowen, Philad.ᵃ

On Stone by W.E. Hitchcock

Red-tailed Squirrel.

Drawn from Nature by J.J. Audubon, F.R.S.F.L.S   Lith. Printed & Col.d by J.T. Bowen, Philada

Drawn on Stone by Wᵐ E. Hitchcock

Richardson's Columbian Squirrel

Drawn from Nature by J.J.Audubon, F.R.S.F.L.S.   Lith. Printed & Colᵈ. by J.T.Bowen, Phil.

N.º 18.

Plate LXXXIX

On Stone by Wᵐ E Hitchcock

Lith. Printed & Colᵈ by J.T.Bowen, Philad

Say's Squirrel

Drawn from Nature by J.J.Audubon,F.R.S.P.L.S.

Soft haired Squirrel.

Drawn from Nature by J.J. Audubon F.R.S.F.L.S.   Printed by Nagel & Weingærtner, N.Y.

Drawn on Stone by R. Trembly.

Fig 1

Fig. 2.

Drawn on Stone by Wm. E. Hitchcock.

Fig.1 *Weasel - like Squirrel*

Fig.2. *Large Louisiana Black Squirrel.*

Drawn from Nature by J.W. Audubon.   Lith. Printed & Col.d by J.T. Bowen, Phil

Drawn from Nature by J.J.Audubon F.R.S, F.L.S.

Drawn on Stone by R.Trembly.

Cotton Rat.

Printed by Nagel & Weingærtner NY

Plate CXXV

Drawn from Nature by J.W.Audubon.

Lith. Printed & Col.d by J.T.Bowen.Phil.

American Marsh Shrew

632

Plate LXXV.

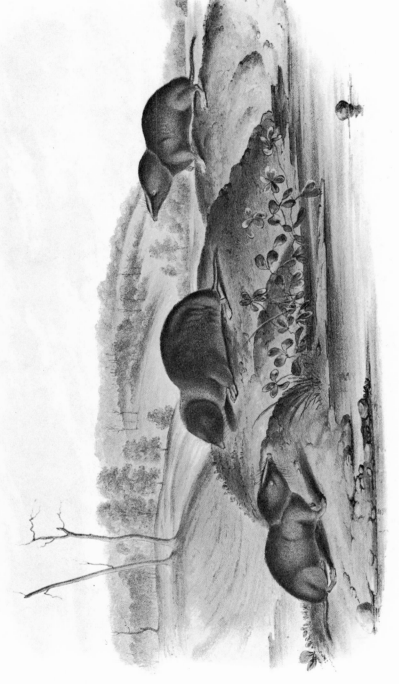

On Stone by Wᵐ E. Hitchcock

Drawn from Nature by J J Audubon, F R S F L S

Lith. Printed & Colᵈ by J T Bowen Phil.

Carolina Shrew

Nº 14

Plate LXX.

Drawn from Nature by J.J. Audubon, F.R.S.F.L.S.

On Stone by Wᵐ E. Hitchcock

Say's Least Shrew.

Lith. Printed & Col⁴ by J T. Bowen, Philad

Plate LXXIX

Drawn from Nature by J.J.Audubon, FRSFL S

On Stone by Wᵐ. E. Hitchcock.

Lith. Printed & Colᵈ by J.T Bowen, Phil.

Annulated Marmot Squirrel.

Drawn from Nature by J.J. Audubon F.R.S.F.L.S.

Douglasses Spermophile.

Lith. Printed & Cold by J.T. Bowen Philada

On stone. by W.E. Hitchcock

Lith.ᵈ Printed & Col.ᵈ by J.I.Bowen Philad.ᵃ

Drawn from Nature by J.J.Audubon F.R.S.Fl.S.

Franklin's Marmot Squirrel.

No. 31

Plate CLIV

Fig 1

Fig 2

Drawn from Nature by J. W. Audubon.

On Stone by Wm F. Hitchcock

Lith. Printed & Cold by J.T. Bowen, Phil

Fig 1 Harris' Marmot-Squirrel   Fig 2 California Meadow-Mouse

Plate XXXIX.

Drawn on Stone by R. Trembly

Drawn from Nature by J.J. Audubon, F.R.S. F.L.S

Leopard Spermophile.

Lith. Printed & Col⁴ by J T Bowen, Ph.

Drawn from Nature by J.W. Audubon

On Stone by W.E. Hitchcock

Lith Printed & Cold by J.T. Bowen, Philada.

Large - tailed Spermophile

Plate. CIX

Drawn on Stone by Wᵐ E. Hitchcock

Mexican Marmot Squirrel.

Adult male and young

Drawn from Nature by J.W.Audubon.

Lith. Printed & Col⁵by. T.Bowen, Phil

Drawn from Nature by J.J.Audubon,F.R.S.F.L.S

On Stone by Wm E. Hitchcock

Lith. Printed & Cold by J.T. Bowen, Phil

Parry's Marmot Squirrel

Plate XCIX.

On Stone by Wm. E. Hitchcock

Drawn from Nature by J.J.Audubon, F.R.S.F.L.S.

Lith. Printed & Cold by J.T. Bowen, Phil.

Prairie Dog.— Prairie Marmot Squirrel.

Plate L.

Drawn from Nature by J.J.Audubon. F.R.S.F.L.S.

Richardson's Spermophile

Lith⁴ Printed & Col⁴ by J.T. Bowen, Philad.ᵃ

No. 23

Plate CXIV.

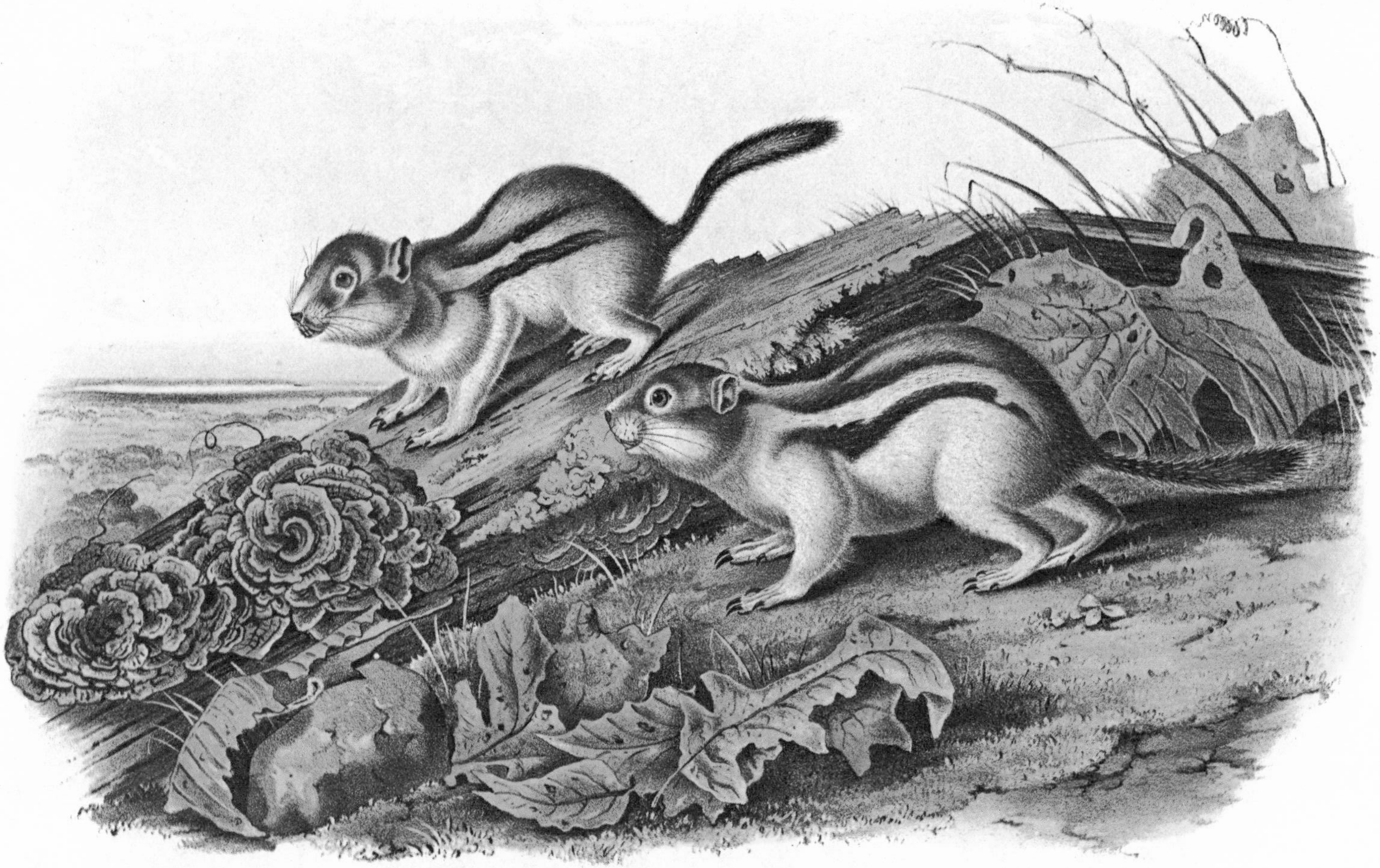

Drawn on stone by W. E. Hitchcock

Drawn from Nature by J. W. Audubon

Say's Marmot Squirrel.

Lith. Printed & Col.d by J. T. Bowen, Philada.

Drawn on Stone by R. Trembly

Chipping Squirrel, Hackee.

Drawn from Nature by J.J.Audubon F.R.S, F.L.S.

Printed by Nagel & Weingærtner N.Y

Plate XXIV

Drawn on Stone by R. Trembly

Four striped Ground Squirrel.
1. Male, 2 Female, 3 & 4. Young.

Drawn from Nature by J. J. Audubon F.R.S., F.L.S.

Printed by Nagel & Weingärtner NY

Townsend's Ground Squirrel

Drawn from Nature by J J Audubon F R S F L S

Drawn on Stone by R Trembly

Printed by Nagel & Weingärtner N.Y.

Colored by J Lawrence

Plate CXLI

N° 22.

Drawn from Nature by J. W. Audubon

On Stone by W. E. Hitchcock

American Black Bear

Lith. Printed & Col. by J. T. Bowen, Phil.

Plate CXXVII.

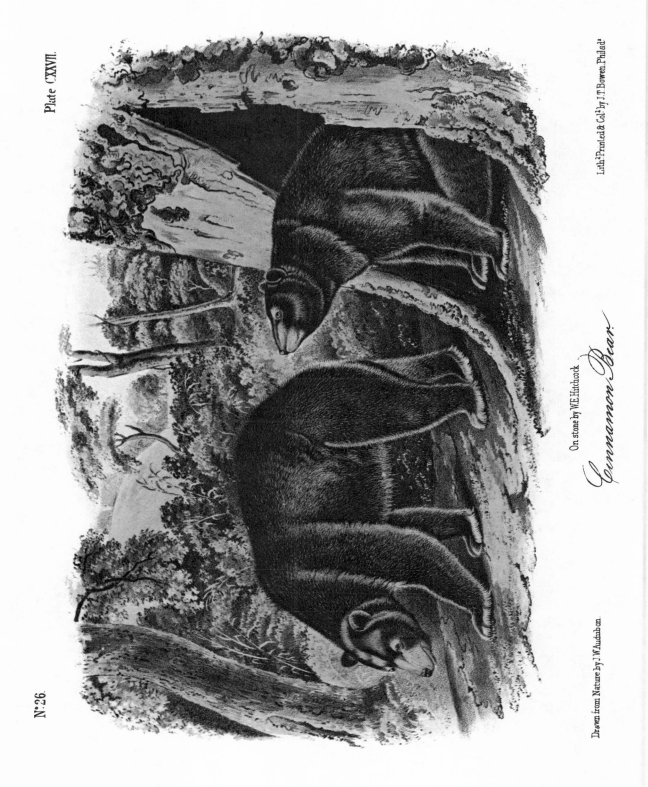

On stone by W.E.Hitchcock.

Lith⁴.Printed & Col⁴.by J.T.Bowen.Philad⁴.

Cinnamon Bear.

Drawn from Nature by J.W.Audubon.

N°27.

Plate CXXXI.

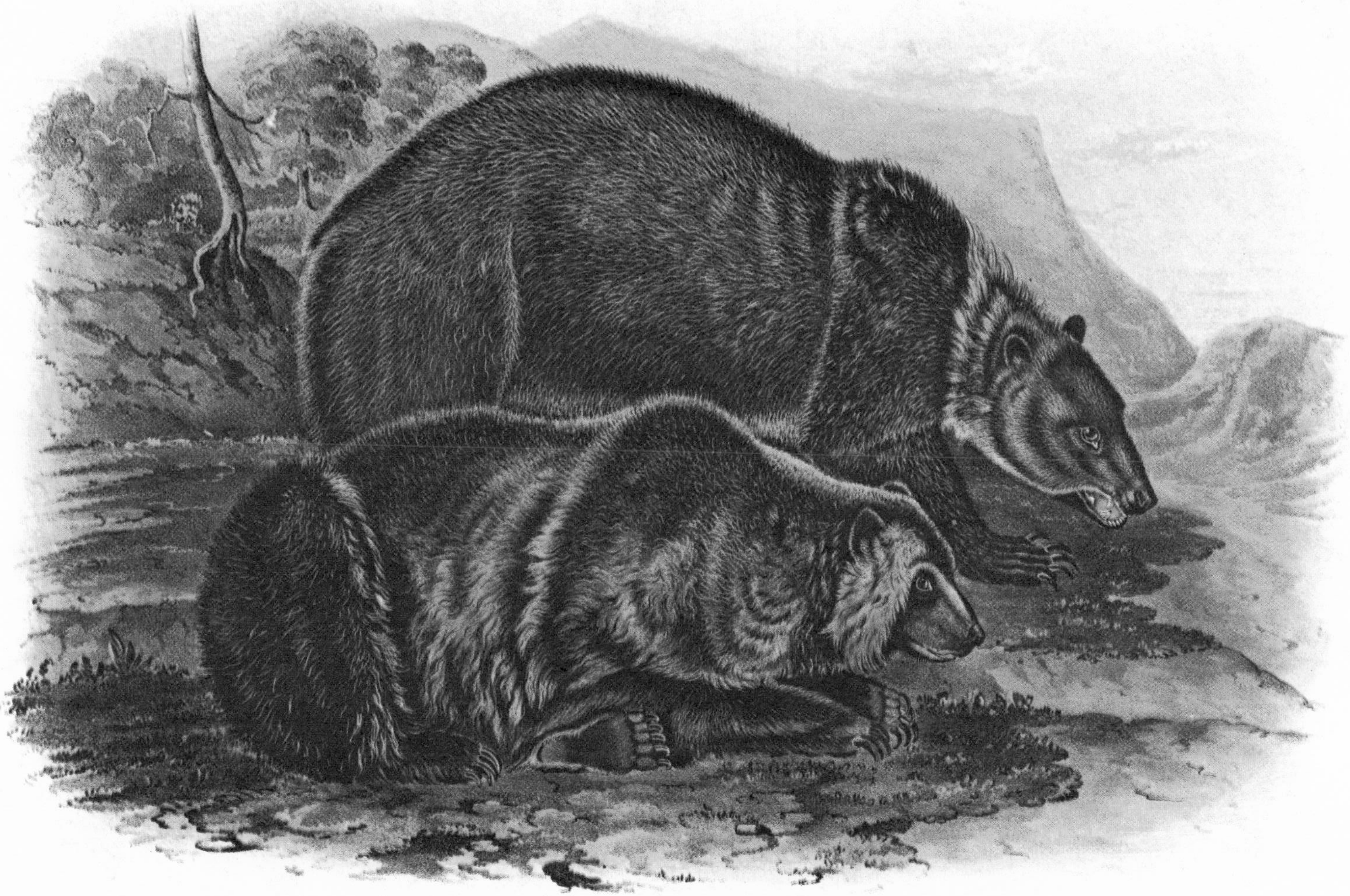

On stone by W.E.Hitchcock

Drawn from Nature by J. W. Audubon

Grizzly Bear.

Lith Printed & Col.d by J. T. Bowen, Philad.

Plate XCI

On Stone by Wm E Hitchcock

Polar Bear.

Lith. Printed & Cold by J.T. Bowen

N° 24. Plate CXVI.

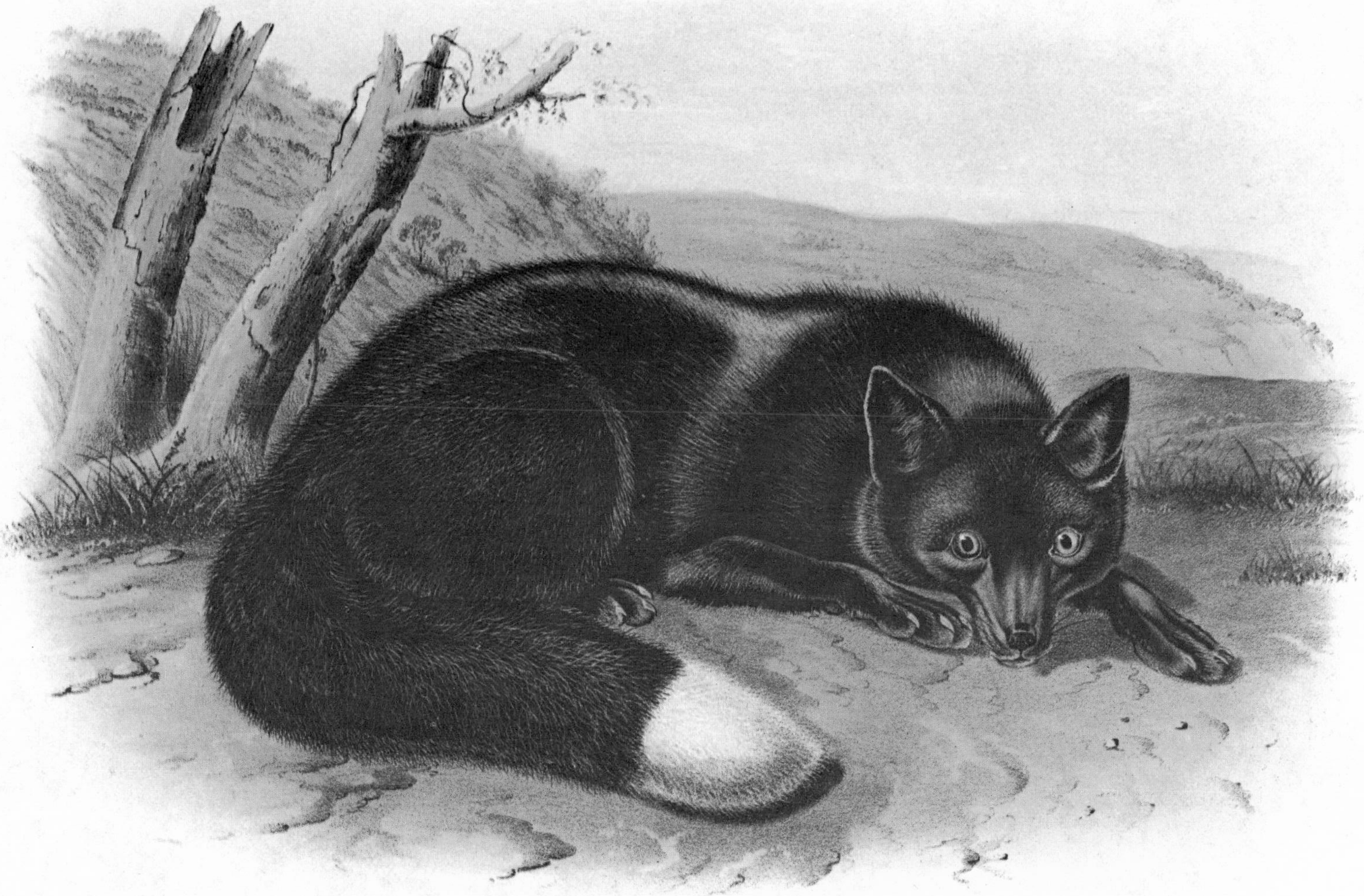

On Stone by W.E. Hitchcock.

Drawn from Nature by J.W. Audubon. Lith.d Printed & Col.d by J.T. Bowen, Philad.a

American Black or Silver Fox.

Plate VI

Drawn from Nature by J.J. Audubon F.R.S. F.L.S.
Drawn on Stone by R.Trembly

American Cross Fox.

Printed by Nagel & Weingärtner N.Y.

Plate LXXXVII.

Drawn from Nature by J.J.Audubon, F.R.S.F.L.S.   On Stone by Wm E.Hitchcock   Lith Printed & Col.d by J.T.Bowen, Phil.ad   *American Red-Fox.*

Drawn on Stone by Wm E. Hitchcock.

Arctic Fox.

Drawn from Nature by J W Audubon.

Lith. Printed & Col.ᵈ by J T Bowen Phil

Plate XXI

No. 5

Drawn from Nature by J.J.Audubon F.R.S.F.L.S.

Gray Fox.
Male.

Printed by Nagel & Weingärtner N.Y.

No. 31

Plate CLI

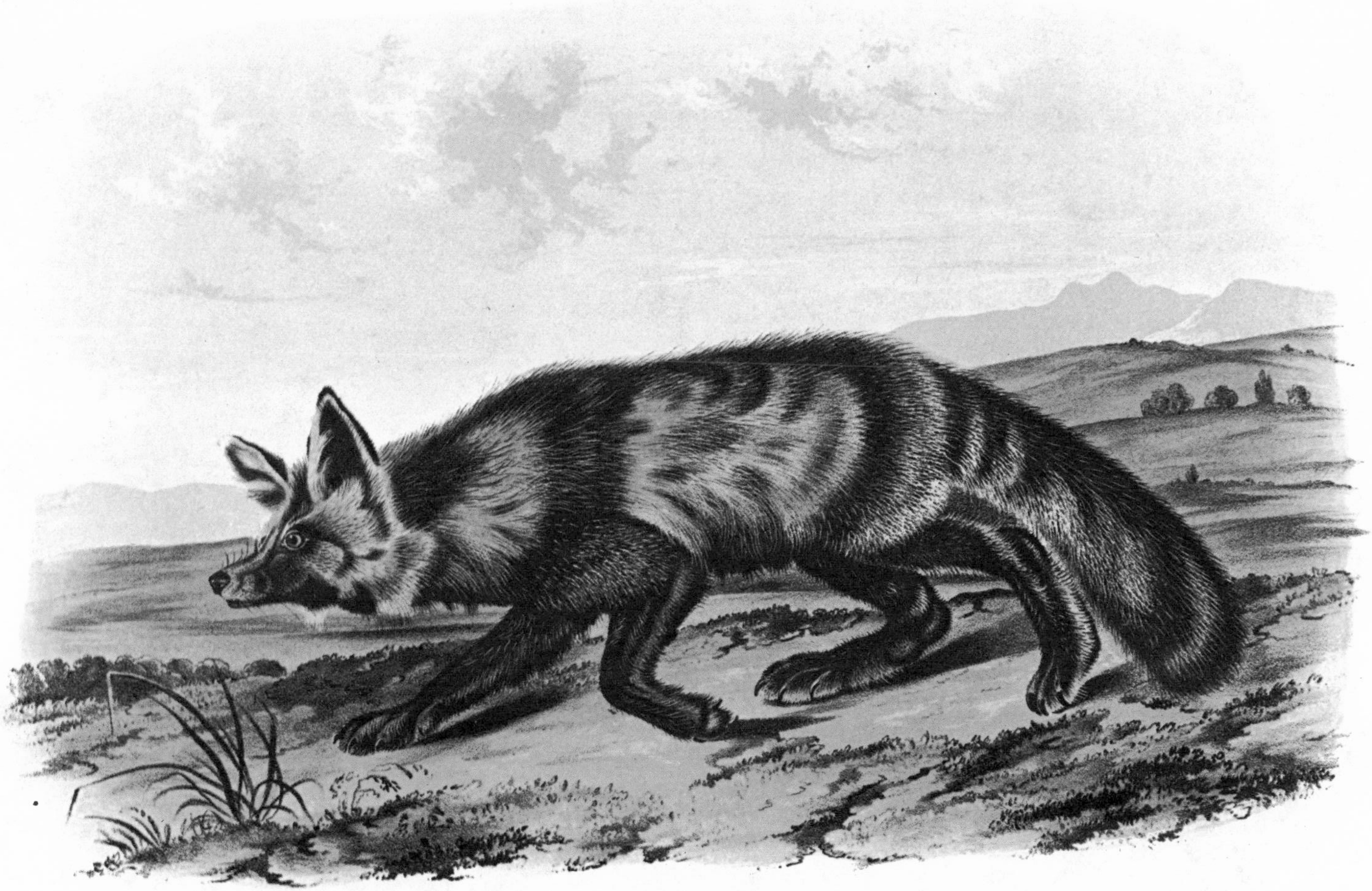

On Stone by Wm. E. Hitchcock

Drawn from Nature by J.W. Audubon

Lith. Printed & Col.d by J.T. Bowen, Phil

Jackall Fox.

N° 11. Plate LII

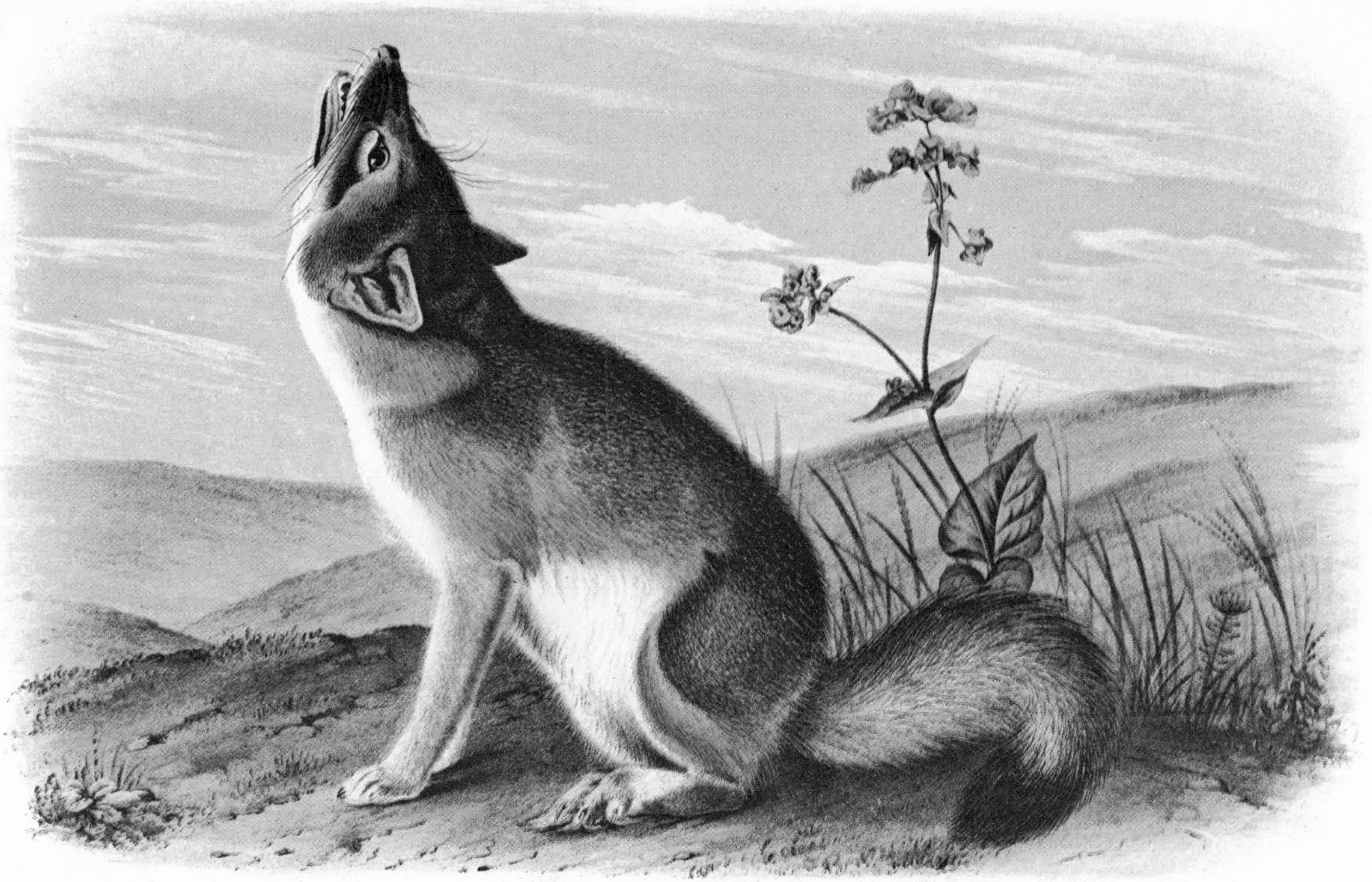

Drawn on Stone by Wm E. Hitchcock.

Swift Fox.

Drawn from Nature by J. J. Audubon, F.R.S. F.L.S.

Lith. Printed & Col^d^ by J. T. Bowen, Philada

Index

BIRDS—LATIN–ENGLISH

Wolf, Red Texan	Canis lupus (var. rufus)	525
Wolf, White American	Canis griseus	526
Wolverine	Gulo luscus	549
Woodchuck	Arctomys monax	509

MAMMALS—LATIN-ENGLISH

Antilocapra Americana	Prong-Horned Antelope	505
Aplondontia leporina	Sewellel	506
Arctomys flaviventer	Yellow-Bellied Marmot	510
Arctomys Lewisii	Lewis' Marmot	508
Arctomys monax	Woodchuck	509
Arctomys pruinosus	Hoary Marmot	507
Arvicola borealis	Northern Meadow Mouse	512
Arvicola edax	Harris' Marmot Spermophile	638
Arvicola edax see Spermophilus Harrisii		
Arvicola nasuta	Sharp-Nosed Arvicola	515
Arvicola Oregoni	Oregon Meadow Mouse	513
Arvicola Oregoni see Spermophilus Townsendii		
Arvicola orizivora	Bank Rat	515
Arvicola Pennsylvanica	Wilson's Meadow Mouse	516
Arvicola pinetorum	Le Conte's Pine Mouse	511
Arvicola Richardsonii	Richardson's Meadow Mouse	514
Arvicola Texiana	Texan Meadow Mouse	513
Arvicola Texiana see Spermophilus Townsendii		
Arvicola Townsendii	Townsend's Arvicola	515
Arvicola xanthognatha	Yellow-Cheeked Meadow Mouse	517
Bassaris astuta	Ring-Tailed Bassaris	518
Bison Americanus	Buffalo	519, 520
Canis familiaris (var. borealis)	Esquimaux Dog	522
Canis familiaris (var. lagopus)	Hare-Indian Dog	523
Canis griseus	White American Wolf	526
Canis latrans	Prairie Wolf	524
Canis lupus (var. ater)	Black American Wolf	521
Canis lupus (var. rufus)	Red Texan Wolf	525
Capra Americana	Rocky Mountain Goat	527
Castor fiber (var. Americanus)	American Beaver	528
Cervus alces	Moose Deer	534
Cervus leucurus	Long-Tailed Deer	533
Cervus macrotis	Black-Tailed Deer	529
Cervus Richardsonii	Columbian Black-Tailed Deer	530
Cervus Virginianus	Common American Deer	531, 532
Condylura cristata	Common Star-Nosed Mole	535
Dasypus peba	Nine-Banded Armadillo	536

Didelphis Virginiana	Virginian Opossum	537
Dipodomys Phillipsii	Pouched Jerboa Mouse	538
Dycotyles torquatus	Collared Peccary	539
Elaphus Canadensis	American Elk	540
Enhydra marina	Sea Otter	541
Felis concolor	Cougar (Female & Young)	542
Felis concolor	Cougar (Male)	543
Felis onca	Jaguar	544
Felis pardalis	Ocelot	545
Fiber zibethicus	Muskrat	546
Georychus helvolus	Tawny Lemming	548
Georychus Hudsonius	Hudson's Bay Lemming	547
Georychus trimucronatus	Back's Lemming	548
Gulo luscus	Wolverine	549
Hystrix dorsata	Canada Porcupine	550
Lagomys princeps	Little Chief Hare	551
Lepus Americanus	Northern Hare (Summer Pelage)	557
Lepus Americanus	Northern Hare (Winter Pelage)	558
Lepus aquaticus	Swamp Hare	561
Lepus artemesia	Worm-Wood Hare	564
Lepus Bachmani	Bachman's Hare	522
Lepus Californicus	Californian Hare	554
Lepus glacialis	Polar Hare	560
Lepus nigricaudatus	Black-Tailed Hare	553
Lepus Nuttalii	Nuttall's Hare	559
Lepus palustris	Marsh Hare	556
Lepus sylvaticus	Grey Rabbit	555
Lepus Texianus	Texan Hare	562
Lepus Townsendii	Townsend's Rocky Mountain Hare	563
Lutra Canadensis	Canada Otter	565, 566
Lynx Canadensis	Canada Lynx	567
Lynx rufus	Common American Wildcat	568
Lynx rufus (var. maculatus)	Texan Lynx	569
Meles Labradoria	American Badger	570
Mephitis chinga	Common American Skunk	571
Mephitis macroura	Large-Tailed Skunk	572
Mephitis mesoleuca	Texan Skunk	573
Meriones Hudsonicus	Jumping Mouse	574
Mus (calomys) aureolus	Orange-Colored Mouse	581
Mus decumanus	Norway Rat	577
Mus humilis	Little Harvest Mouse	579
Mus leucopus	American White-Footed Mouse	575
Mus Missouriensis	Missouri Mouse	580
Mus musculus	Common Mouse	578
Mus rattus	Black Rat	576
Mustela Canadensis	Pennant's Marten	582
Mustela martes	Pine Marten	583
Neotoma Drummondii	Rocky Mountain Neotoma	585
Neotoma Floridana	Florida Rat	584
Ovibos moschatus	Musk-Ox	586